ANY MUDDY BOTTOM

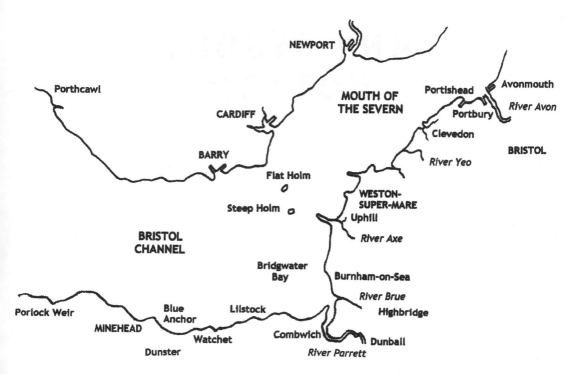

NEWPORT

Porthcawl

MOUTH OF
THE SEVERN

Portishead   Avonmouth

CARDIFF   River Avon
                                Portbury

                        Clevedon   BRISTOL

BARRY
                Flat Holm
                                River Yeo

                Steep Holm   WESTON-
                                SUPER-MARE
                                Uphill

BRISTOL   River Axe
CHANNEL

                        Bridgwater   Burnham-on-Sea
                        Bay
                                River Brue

Porlock Weir   Blue   Lilstock   Highbridge
                Anchor
        MINEHEAD   Combwich
                Watchet   Dunball

        Dunster   River Parrett

ANY MUDDY BOTTOM

A HISTORY OF SOMERSET'S WATERBORNE TRADE

GEOFF BODY AND ROY GALLOP

Cover illustrations: *Front*: Highbridge Wharf pictured in late Victorian years; *Rear*: At the lowest point of the tide a steam collier sits on the mud alongside the upper reach of Highbridge Wharf.

First published 2015

The History Press
The Mill, Brimscombe Port
Stroud, Gloucestershire, GL5 2QG
www.thehistorypress.co.uk

British Library Cataloguing in Publication Data.
A catalogue record for this book is available from the British Library.

ISBN 978 0 7509 6163 9

Typesetting and origination by The History Press
Printed in Great Britain

CONTENTS

INTRODUCTION, ACKNOWLEDGEMENTS AND SOURCES

This is how it all came about. The day was warm, the sky unclouded and the open countryside below the Quantocks had a freshness to it only to be found in springtime. Suitably refreshed by lunch in Stogursey, we drove towards the Somerset coast, intent on a leisurely exploration of an area we had not previously visited. Near Lilstock, we came upon a small parking area behind a stretch of higher ground and responded to the temptation to follow a gentle footpath and its companion stream in the general direction of the widening Bristol Channel.

Nothing seemed in the least unusual until we rounded a bluff and emerged onto a wide-topped shingle bank and a view of the calm, sand-tinged coastal waters. On the other side of the channel lay the Welsh coastline on either side of Barry, the whole a quiet, peaceful and idyllic location. However, noticeable on our right was a substantial and unusual grassy indentation, parallel to the shingle bank and between it and the modest rise of the higher ground beyond.

Intrigued, we scrambled down the slope to explore the dip further. It was quite long and interest mounted as parting the fringe vegetation revealed the high quality masonry of what must originally have been long, low walls. More observant now, we continued to the eastern end of the indentation and spotted more masonry on either side. Suddenly it all became clear. These had to be the remains of what would once have been the supports for lock gates. We were standing inside what could only have been a former dock, and one of quite significant proportions, extremely surprising considering its remote location.

Stretching into the sea nearby were the remains of a breakwater and, deep in the undergrowth beyond the dock entrance, lay further surprise in the form of the use-blackened masonry of sizeable twin limekilns. This must have been a busy place at one time.

This unplanned beginning led to a story, uncovered further in the *Victoria County History* and other places, of a former dock which had been built originally to receive coal for estate hearths and limekilns. It had been of some significance and at one time as many as three sailing vessels would have been moored up there. A social mini-drama added another dimension in which a short pier became a picnic spot and health-giving social venue and later a calling point for channel steamers.

Roy's experience in sailing the waters of the Bristol Channel and beyond had, at this period, found a land based expression in a programme of illustrated lectures on the 'lost ports' of Gloucestershire and Somerset. My first hardback book had been on the subject of British paddle steamers and we had jointly studied both the Glastonbury Canal and the Parrett Navigation and published booklets on these subjects. This common interest in water transport was behind our delight in our new Lilstock discovery.

Our *Town Trail* articles for the old *Somerset Magazine* had given us a nodding acquaintance with the main Somerset harbours but now, fired by our visit to this half-hidden dock, we set about finding more information on the whole subject. So far as we could discover, the story of the ports, vessels and trade of the Somerset coast and waterways had been covered quite widely, but only piecemeal. Grahame Farr's *Somerset Harbours* is a warm and interesting treatment of its subject, and there have been detailed accounts of sailing voyages, Bristol's early trade, the Parrett salt trade, Bridgwater docks and other such specifics. The gap which this work endeavours to fill is that of an over-the-centuries look at the whole waterborne trade, the vessels that carried it, the people who manned and sailed them, what they actually did on a day-to-day basis and what factors prompted and shaped the activity.

We are grateful for the assistance we have had in this task in studying material at the Somerset Record Office, the Somerset Local Studies Library, main libraries in the coastal areas, various learned papers, local history writings and from the many individuals who have contributed information on the subject during our talks and wanderings. For any gaps and errors we are sorry, but have no regrets over attempting this endeavour.

The photographs, drawings and other illustrations appearing in this work come from the collections of the authors themselves except where specifically acknowledged.

Specific sources include: the *Victoria County History, Somerset Harbours* (Grahame Farr, Christopher Johnson, London, 1954), *Ships and Harbours of Exmoor* (Grahame Farr, The Exmoor Press, 1970), *Out of Appledore* (W.J. Slade, Percival Marshall & Co Ltd, London, 1959), *Sailing Craft of the British Isles* (Roger Finch, William Collins Sons & Co Ltd, London, 1976), *Bridgwater Docks & the River Parrett* (Brian J. Murless, Somerset County Library, 1983), *Squibbs' History of Bridgwater* (Philip J. Squibbs, Phillimore, 1982), *Minehead: A New History* (Hilary Binding & Douglas Stevens, The Exmoor Press, 1977), *The Westcountrymen: Ketches & Trows of the Bristol Channel* (Gordon Mote, Badger Books, Bideford, 1986), *Lydney Docks* (Neil Parkhouse, Black Dwarf Publications, 2001), *Bristol's Trade with Ireland and the Continent, 1503–1601* (Susan Flavin & Evan T. Jones, Four Courts Press for the Bristol Record Society, 2009), *The Eroder Boats of the Somerset Levels* (Mary Miles, Bulletins of the Somerset Industrial Archaeological Society Nos 61–3).

Special thanks are due to Amy Rigg, Lauren Newby and the team at The History Press, and to Ian Body, Tess Green and David Pochin.

A CARGO OF COAL

Recreates a typical journey by a ketch carrying a load of coal from the Forest of Dean pits destined for the cement works adjacent to Dunball Wharf near Bridgwater.

Transport yourself back to the nineteenth century. Great changes have been happening, accelerating rapidly and accompanied in the area of the Bristol Channel by the building and expansion of the docks for the export of coal from South Wales and the railways linking them with the inland valleys and their mines. Coal had overtaken the original Welsh iron industries in importance and now went all over Britain and, indeed, all over the world. It fed not only domestic hearths and industries, but passed in quantity to naval bases like Portland and onward to bunkering depots on all the major shipping routes. To move the coal output from South Wales and the Forest of Dean more railways had been opened to create links with and facilitate great expansion in the Midlands. Their tracks had first crossed the River Severn by a bridge from Lydney to Sharpness and then tunnelled under it near Chepstow to improve the routes between the Welsh and Dean pits and the ever-growing demand in London and from the ports along the South Coast.

The River Severn itself had changed; steam tugs had appeared in the 1830s, followed by navigation improvements a decade later. Even so, the railway intrusion had greatly affected the age-old pattern of small trows depending on the tides in their trading on the Upper and Middle Severn, compelling changes in vessel design and forcing owners to search for new markets in deeper waters to Somerset, Devon and beyond. This upheaval forms the background to our journey.

Our ketch had started life in a boatbuilder's yard at Saul. This area, where the Stroudwater link from the Thames & Severn Canal reached the major artificial waterway paralleling the tidal Severn from Gloucester to Sharpness, was the birthplace of hundreds of such vessels. She had been built some fifty years earlier as a conventional trow with the typical barge-like appearance, open holds and a single mast and square sail to supplement her use of the tides. Her trade had been upriver from Gloucester with woollens and back with salt from Droitwich, but all that had been lost to the better rates and quicker journeys of the traffic-hungry railways.

With the same enterprise rivermen had always shown, her owners and skipper had arranged for a boatyard to cut our trow in two and insert an extra centre section of some 15ft. With her keel strengthened, along with proper sideboards and with hatches covering part of the hold, she could now carry some 120 tons instead of the former 60-ton maximum, and also handle a wider variety of cargoes, including those needing cover. Instead of the previous simple square sail, she was now rigged as a ketch with a bowsprit, main and mizzen masts and the canvas to make good use of them.

A modern view of the tidal basin at Lydney Harbour, now tidied up and nicely landscaped and with little evidence of the former railway lines and coal chutes. Yachts are beached on the adjacent foreshore and Sharpness Docks can be seen on the other side of the River Severn.

To complete our vessel's transformation, one of the new marine engines had only recently been installed. This would help immensely in improving control and journey times when favourable winds were not to be had. It did mean that the crew had been forced to move from the aft cabin, such as it was, for slightly less roomy shelter in the forecastle. But seamen are used to adapting to circumstances and new homes had been found for all the loose gear, together with places for the essential bunks, stove and food supplies.

On the occasion of this imaginary but typical voyage, we were going to take advantage of our new capacity. Our staple traffic was Forest of Dean coal to feed the kilns of the cement works at Dunball, with a load of bricks from Bridgwater in the other direction. Now, however, we could use the new hold capacity and our ability to section the fore and aft portions to advantage. We intended to load the main contract tonnage of coal in the centre hold, stow a smaller load for the local farmer-cum-coal merchant aft and yet another small load for'ard, the latter destined to be sent on by Great Western Railway goods train from Dunball to Exeter. All these movements had been going on for years, that to Exeter even going back to Great Western Railway broad gauge days and the regular 'Old Coal Train' working, but they would previously have required two vessels to handle our present load.

We were loading at Lydney, which was a good little port and the cheapest along the Lower Severn. The coal that came from the nearest inland mines worked by the Free Miners of the Forest went southwards down the Severn in the main. Those northern flows not lost to the trains usually went through Lydbrook for places reached via the River Wye, while those for more northerly Severn destinations were transferred from wagon to vessel at the Great Western Railway's loading point at Bullo Pill.

Dean coal also crossed the river from west to east. Some of it went to Sharpness Docks for use, bunkering and other purposes there. Other flows joined the Gloucester & Sharpness Canal and went on to fuel Cadbury's factory or continue to Gloucester Docks. Loads for Stroud and the Thames & Severn Canal turned east again at Saul.

Whatever the destination, Lydney Pill, which had been the original outlet for a modest coal canal, then a tram road and then a proper railway, was now a well-run port, complete with inner and outer basins, rail sidings and wagon-tipping chutes.

The day before our trip back to the Bristol Channel, we had entered Lydney Harbour without difficulty, now a much easier process with an engine to give us controllable steerage way. Without this we would have had to wait for slack water or risk being swept onto the sands downstream of the pier. Thanks also to our engine, gone was the difficult task of coming alongside the right-hand quay of the outer basin and taking way off the vessel by slipping the hawser over a bollard, but controlling the tightening so as not to rip the other end out of the deck. We still had to judge our moment for at really busy times there might be fifty or more vessels at Lydney, giving the harbour master a real berthing headache.

We had got rid of our load of bricks to waiting carts on the north side of the inner basin and even managed to sweep out the hold before the last of daylight. The bricks were for local use so there had been no help for it but to unload manually with our well-worn barrows. Now seriously tired, we opted against the walk along the canal into Lydney proper in favour of a leisurely brew and satisfying fry-up on the boat. We always stocked up before each voyage from the little shop at Dunball, based on a fairly standard list of bacon, eggs, sausages, potatoes, onions, bread, milk, tea, cheese, jam and bread. The choice depended

The last major traffic movement through Lydney Harbour was this flow of West African timber, towed up in barges from Avonmouth Docks for use at Pine End Works which was located on the canal between the dock entrance and Lydney town. The plywood produced there had been used to build aircraft during the war, but the intake of materials was eventually transferred to road in 1977 to end a long waterborne connection and effectively close the dock.

on our schedule and had porridge as a regular extra in colder weather. By the time we had enjoyed our meal, tidied up afterwards and settled down for a chat, a smoke and a glass of beer with a few other boatmen, the two cramped and spartan bunks seemed very inviting.

We had an early start the next day and had to hurry breakfast, but at least it was not raining. After turning beyond the inner set of dock gates we were now awaiting our turn for one of the several loading chutes. The normal division of duties was for the captain to see to the procedures and provisioning, checking the cargo paperwork, paying the harbour dues and the like. The mate's job was to make sure that our wagons were actually where they should be and to find out which chute was to be used. A chat with the railway foreman made sure they would be moved into position along the raised line of track by the shunting engine or the capstan man.

The whole operation of the port reflected the tide table for, not blessed with the modest latitude our engine gave us, many users still had no auxiliary power and relied entirely on the ebbing tide to take them down river. Exit through the lock gates to the tidal basin could be a crowded operation because of this need to catch the tide and was one requiring careful vessel control and queuing.

For the moment all that mattered was that both our vessel and our railway wagons were in position on time. Each 10-ton load had to be turned on the wagon turntable, run out onto the short pier to bring it over and beside the vessel and then tilted by counterbalance and hand winch to allow the wagon end door to swing open and the load to come rushing down the chute and into the hold. It was not a rapid operation, especially as we had to move the vessel along to distribute the load, even if two chutes were in use. And that meant either some hard pulling on the bow rope or finding a handy capstan. A cloud of dust was inevitable and one of the many discomforts of our life. However, we could now afford the 4*d* a ton for trimmers to level the load evenly, thanks to the cost of our new engine being paid for out of the savings we made by not having to use the pier hauling crew to tow us out of the basin or paying for a steam tug to do so.

Loading completed and the hatch covers secured, we signalled our readiness to leave and took our turn in passing through the outer basin gates and heading for the river, snatching an occasional glance at the scene astern where half a dozen towing men were straining to get an unengined vessel moving. They continued their daunting task along the pier which stretches into the river on the upstream side of the harbour so that their charge had enough headway to catch the tide ebbing past the pier head and be swept off downstream. Passage of the Severn was always tricky, with tidal speeds varying from neap rates of 2 to 3 knots to spring rates of 10 knots and with the tidal rise and fall in the lower reaches as much as 39m in the latter. Timing and vigilance were critical.

We, too, had taken advantage of a good tide and, by doing so, could save fuel and need not even hoist the sails until we were near the junction of the Wye and Severn rivers at Beachley. Still, it was good to have the engine in reserve. Even to a man bred to sail, the steady thump of it at work when needed was a reassuring sound. We still had to exercise great care, though, in the passage downriver, taking an east bank course past Berkeley and Oldbury and keeping well away from the rocks off Aust.

With the wind now favourable we hoisted sail, always conscious that fuel was expensive and limited our use of the engine to when it was really needed. Vigilance was especially important on this stretch passing through The Shoots, the tricky final bottleneck before reaching the widening estuary and the Bristol Channel beyond. There was only a narrow, 300-yard gap between Gruggy Rock and the English Stones and we were not the only ones heading for it. Eddies and whirlpools were a feature of these particular waters and could cause real problems under sail when the wind was not sufficient to give the hull and rudder a decent 'bite' on the water. At difficult times the ship's boat might have to be launched and used to guide the head. Fog was sometimes a nightmare here and would give me an extra job of ringing our bell, but today with the skipper at the tiller and me trimming the sails – both keeping a watchful eye out – there were no problems.

Unless the wind became unreliable or contrary we could, after this tricky stretch, usually get most of the way to our destination under sail, normally following the deeper channel along the Welsh coast and avoiding the sometimes turbulent waters between Flat Holm and Steep Holm. There was a lot more activity on this stretch, often crowded with tugs, pleasure steamers and colliers, motor vessels and barges, together with a host of other craft still dependent on sail. The traffic included quite large vessels heading to or from Avonmouth or the South Wales ports and too dependent on an adequate depth of water to defer to those with a shallower draught.

In the best of circumstances the turn of the tide would help us across the channel and into the mouth of the River Parrett without the risk of grounding in some of the shallower places around Stert Island. Gone were the days when we might have spent a lot of time waiting on the tides to get up river. We were now less dependent on both tide and tugs. It was time to restart the engine and, once safely into the estuary, we continued under power up the river, but it was not yet time to relax our watch-keeping. We needed to keep a good lookout along its winding course, not only because its depths were constantly changing, but for the low-lying flatners and other fishing vessels which were about in numbers and not always easy to spot. Sully's tug *Bonita* was just dropping off a ketch at the Chilton brickworks and there were others at Combwich where the ferry always seemed to be trying to cross as we passed.

Dunball Reach and our destination at last. A careful turn across the river would bring us alongside the railway wharf at Dunball with the bow pointing downstream and the stern nicely brought in line by the tide, a procedure which also took way off the vessel. Without our engine this river transit might have taken several tides to accomplish. What a difference it now made to the difficulties we used to meet in all those places with a tortuous approach or where the kedge or heavy anchor had to be rowed out on the ebb tide to help in getting off after the load had been discharged!

This drawing from an old photograph shows the trow *Mary* in Dunball Pill. *Mary* was a frequent visitor to the River Parrett and her cargo would have been Forest of Dean coal, most likely from Lydney. As can be seen in the picture this trow had an open hold with no hatch covers. (Roy Gallop)

It had been a good trip and our ketch would now settle nicely on the bottom which, for many years, was kept level by the crew of mud rakers employed by the railway. With everything made fast we could tidy up, cross the dock to the Greenhill Arms to relax in its cider room and then head for home. Tomorrow the wharf cranes would remove most of our cargo, either directly into railway wagons for transfer to the cement works or working forward to more distant destinations, or to the carts of the local farmer-cum-coal merchant. Thank goodness we no longer had to do this by the age-old shovel and basket method. Clearing the bottom dust ready for our next load was bad enough without having to 'walk the plank' with a loaded wheelbarrow!

Our vessel had done us proud and, although she still had something of the solid look of her trow origins, she had taken well to her new life with ketch rig and marine engine and we both had a real affection for her.

PART 1

Coastal Sailing Trade

1. FROM PILL TO PORLOCK

Somerset has a long coastline which stretches from the mouth of the River Avon to the Devon border. South-west at first along the Severn Estuary, heading for Clevedon and Weston-super-Mare, it then forms the English shore of the Bristol Channel around Bridgwater Bay, before turning west to Watchet, Minehead and Porlock Bay until it finally reaches the county border with its Devon neighbour. Mostly relatively low-lying, there are also some inhospitable sections of low cliffs, both exposed to the prevailing south-westerly winds that sweep in from the distant Atlantic. Shelter from bad weather is limited and in simpler times placed a high premium on places protected by a headland or other natural feature.

One major river, the Parrett, feeds into the Bristol Channel via Bridgwater and the same part of the coastline has several other significant watercourses, either natural ones like the River Brue or wide drainage channels such as King's Sedgemoor Drain and the Huntspill River. Great changes began in the nineteenth century as part of solving the flooding problems of the Somerset Levels and a number of original river channels were modified in the process. North Somerset has its own drainage-driven network with rivers such as the Axe, the Yeo group and the Banwell, and numerous lesser waterways also drain the higher ground in the west of the county. Everywhere rhynes, sluices and floodgates are a noticeable and vital feature, essential to the balance between disposing of land water and resisting the dramatic tidal variations the coastline experiences.

The estuary of the River Severn together with its seaward continuation, the Bristol Channel, is one huge seawater funnel which unites the flow of its rivers with the deeper waters leading to the Irish Sea. The influence of the Atlantic Ocean and this funnel shape combine to make the tidal range awesome, the second highest in the world. Added to this basic factor is the prevailing south-

The mouth of the River Axe at Uphill typifies the Somerset coast, displaying plenty of mud, a small pill wandering off and the gaunt heights of Brean Down in the background. If a nineteenth-century scheme had succeeded, a deep sea harbour would have been built at the end of the promontory.

westerly wind, the two sometimes producing a combination in which huge seas pound on the headlands and drench the unwary on resort promenades. In earlier times there were frequent inundations of the coastal areas with great floods such as those early in the eighteenth century which swamped large areas of low-lying land and caused the death of both animals and people.

And, as if that was not enough, the funnel has a dog-leg shape which complicates the normal processes of sedimentary scouring and deposit which occur with the ebb and flow of every tide. As a result, not only do water depths vary from place to place, but are not consistent in any one location. In mid-channel the Holm islands produce their own minor water pattern and several areas of the channel reveal huge stretches of sand at the lowest water. Today, of course, the safe navigational course is well marked, but it was not always so.

Emerging from the dramatic Avon Gorge and the following cliff section preceding Pill, the widening River Avon has docks on either side, the older Avonmouth Docks on what was originally the Gloucester side and the new

Portbury Docks on the southern, Somerset side. Beyond the latter a short stretch of marshy land forms a nature reserve. Then, from the pier at the entrance to Portishead Marina and Battery Point at the north end of Portishead's seafront, the estuary starts to widen. An inhospitable rock ledge fronting a stretch of low cliffs takes the Gordano Valley coastline to just beyond Clevedon.

Beyond Clevedon is a stretch of low-lying green meadows whose small waterways emerge into Woodspring Bay. At their southern end the estuary of the Banwell River is followed by the coastline's first major promontory, that of Middle Hope and Sand Point. The next inlet is the modest Sand Bay with Birnbeck and its island at the far end and separating Kewstoke village from Weston Bay and the bustle of the busy seaside resort of Weston-super-Mare.

At the end of Weston-super-Mare's long seafront lies Uphill where a ferry used to cross the mouth of the River Axe to give access to Brean Down, the long, high promontory which marks the gaunt expiry of the Mendip Hills. Still clearly pointing to its former outpost, now Steep Holm Island, this marks a turn of the coastline from south-west to due south along the sands of Brean and Berrow to the Brue and Parrett river mouths.

Leading off the River Axe a small waterway curves round to Uphill village and former wharf. Like so many other similar Somerset locations, its waters are flood controlled by sluice gates.

Summer brings countless families to enjoy the sands of Burnham-on-Sea opposite which Stert Point stretches out into Bridgwater Bay and forms one side of the entrance to the Brue and Parrett rivers. Beyond the point is the vast expanse of Stert Flats, once a serious danger to mariners before the main approach to the Parrett Estuary was properly marked. The coastline of the bay then takes a near right angle course west to Watchet and Minehead in a long section in which mud flats give way first to shingle and black rock shale and then to a further series of low cliffs. Behind the gentle pastureland of the coastal plain stand the magnificent Brendon and Quantock Hills, eventually to be displaced as a backdrop by the heights of Exmoor.

Now in West Somerset, beyond the once-busy harbour at Watchet, are more low cliffs before the sands of Blue Anchor Bay, with Dunster just visible inland, and then the approach to Minehead. There, holiday activities have replaced an age-old involvement in seafaring still marked by the harbour at the western end of the long seafront. Here, steeply rising from North Hill, which shelters Minehead, comes the highest point along the Somerset coast, just over a thousand feet above

Another typical Somerset coastal location, this time Porlock Weir. The pool in the foreground has plenty of water at high tide for access to a tiny dock on the left.

sea level. Where these heights end is Porlock Bay with its shingle foreshore and tiny harbour at Porlock Weir. Some 3 miles further on the high cliffs become part of Devon and the end of the Somerset coastline.

This coastline has shipping traditions that go back to the Phoenicians and the Norse and other invaders, and local fishermen have harvested its waters for as long or longer. Minehead, for example, shipped many a locally-caught herring to less well-placed destinations, not just Bristol, but even to destinations as far away as the Mediterranean ports and sometimes further. Every coastal dweller could depend upon the availability of fresh fish for the table. Minehead was also a licensed pilgrim port, provided vessels to carry supplies in earlier wars and was not above a bit of privateering.

As the centuries moved on the skills of local boatmen became harnessed to trade, and small sailing vessels were kept busy taking county produce to wider markets and bringing both necessities and, increasingly, luxuries in the opposite direction. The vessels they used could often penetrate some way up river and the goods they carried could also move to and from the heart of Somerset after transhipment into barges to work further inland. Equally they might make landfall with a load of culm, the small coal used in estate limekilns, anywhere the bottom was suitable, and then unload the lot by basket and barrow to a lonely shore or the bank of a pill. As a more industrialised society emerged local vessels brought coal from South Wales and the Forest of Dean for both industry and domestic hearth.

The seamen of Somerset became skilled in the use of tides and winds, which could be enemies or friends, and sailed regularly into and up the River Severn, to and from the ports of South Wales, up to Liverpool, to Ireland and Europe and often even further. These hard-working boatmen not only used their home harbour, but were adept at landing and taking on cargoes at any friendly beach or pill as well as trading almost anywhere there was cargo to be had. Their skills were legion and their vessels, some built locally, were long-lived and apt for purpose. Many had numerous owners and chequered careers; shipwrecks and other misadventures were commonplace. All these factors helped to breed the men and vessels who could be called upon in times of war and to steel them to deal with – or even join – the ranks of pirates and privateers and the murky world of smugglers and the customs men who attempted to catch them.

2. THE TRADE ACTIVITY

Trade across and along the Bristol Channel and the Severn Estuary has been going on for centuries. Its make-up has ranged from the age-old movement of produce and livestock to the coals, metals and building materials of the industrial age. The level of shipping activity this trade generated grew in-line with population growth and changed with the varying pattern of agriculture and industry. Until the advent of the canals and railways these waters were a quite vital artery along which small vessels and seasoned sailors linked local producers and consumers to the benefit of both. Overseas trade used the same waters and fishermen followed their craft along the whole coastline. Together they produced a breed of seamen and a tradition of seamanship that stood the nation in good stead in both war and peace. These same seamen showed a remarkable power to adjust to the on-going sequence of change and, despite the growth of the railway system and the huge upheaval it brought, like the effect on trade of the opening of the Severn Bridge and the Severn Tunnel, they adapted and continued to play a major transport role until the 1920s.

The two controlling authorities for the Somerset harbours were the Port of Bristol whose influence stretched from Beachley to Uphill and Bridgwater which controlled the coast on to the Devon border, except for a period when Minehead also enjoyed this special status. Unlike some of the up-channel harbours, Minehead and its satellites at Watchet and Porlock Weir were right on the coast proper, a factor in establishing the sizeable fishing activity of Minehead itself which at one time was sending some sixty barrels of herrings a week to Bristol alone. These were also the harbours nearest to West Wales and the coast beyond, to Ireland and indeed to Europe and the Atlantic Ocean. They also had the advantage of direct access from the open sea as opposed to the upriver location of Bridgwater.

Bridgwater, whose records embraced Combwich and Dunball, may have suffered from a tortuous and limiting approach and had no fishing industry, but it did have one special advantage: a large hinterland, accessible via the River Parrett and its tributaries, and up the River Tone to Taunton. Both were

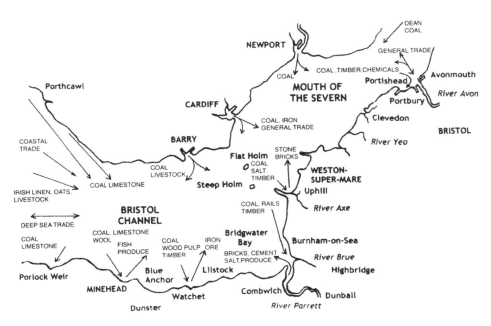

The drawing provides a composite illustration of the principal traffic movements in the Bristol Channel and Severn Estuary. (Roy Gallop)

important access routes for trade to and from inland Somerset and both were supplemented by canalisation and improvements over the years. The River Brue gave access to Highbridge, but the 1833 inland link via the Glastonbury Canal was not a success and Highbridge Wharf owed its existence primarily to its railway ownership and connections. Steam coal and rails, together with timber, were its main traffic.

The Somerset coastal shipping activity was irregular and relatively limited until the huge national changes that followed the Middle Ages. Even so, the Bristol Channel was in regular use as a trade route by vessels from the eleventh century onwards and the early Somerset harbours would at least have had shipping contact with Wales and Ireland. If not great in quantity, the sea transportation of goods was certainly important, the more so because of the limitations of land movement over primitive tracks and through parts liable to winter inundation and flooding. A notable example is an early movement of church furniture from Bristol to Glastonbury which travelled by ship to Uphill and then on via the inland waters of the Pilrow Cut and Meare Pool. As Bristol grew in importance so its requirements for produce increased, and the limitations of land transportation by horse pannier or clumsy wagons prompted regular supply movements in small vessels whenever the weather permitted them to sail.

By the end of the thirteenth century the habit of conflict with Europe, and what is now France, had taken hold and shipping was required to help to prosecute the various wars by carrying troops and supplies. The reality of an organised full-time navy did not emerge until the reign of Henry VIII so that the provision of vessels in wartime was done by requisitioning those normally engaged on more peaceful pursuits. Both Bridgwater and Minehead were called on to contribute vessels of 40 tons or more in 1295 and 1297, presumably because larger vessels from ports nearer the Continent had already been 'enlisted'.

More conflicts followed in the fourteenth century, sometimes demanding the diversion of simple trading vessels, at others confining their activities for fear of invasion. The two main Somerset shipping sources, always Bridgwater and Minehead, both suffered losses in actions from 1369, and the whole process of wartime requisitioning was steadily eroding English maritime strength and resources. For a time the growth in population, towns and commerce was slowed, but it was not to be denied and there was a slow but persistent stirring in the form of a wider vision of the world and its trade possibilities.

Another trend was the rising distinction between the deep sea and coasting trade, as exemplified by the movements to and from La Rochelle. By 1480, for example, Minehead had three vessels working regularly on that route carrying fish and produce one way and wine and salt the other.

The number of ships actually employed in the coasting trade tended to be small with no vessels exceeding 80 tons and the main goods movements being to and from South and West Wales and Ireland. Prominent among these were the flows of limestone pebbles and culm from West Wales to feed and fire the Somerset limekilns, woollen goods both inwards and outwards, surplus products of the Somerset estates and livestock for food and stock purposes. In any event no ships over 100 tons could have reached Bridgwater and nothing at all could pass along the Parrett at the lowest tide times. At this period Dunball Wharf was still in the future and Combwich, although nearer the open sea, did not amount to much more than a pill serving its own immediate locality. For the coasting business, even the regular sailings of produce to and transhipment of goods from Bristol, small single-mast vessels were still the norm, averaging around 40 tons and 45–50ft long. Many even smaller vessels were also to be seen, often carrying loads on an opportunist basis to and from wherever they were available.

More military adventuring emerged from the sixteenth century. If it wasn't the French or Spanish, it was the Dutch. The incentives were less territorial in origin now and more prompted by politics and such causes as the Navigation Acts designed to protect British trade. Whatever the reasons for each war they were now producing an unwelcome maritime by-product. Collectively, they represented an opportunity for incursions by foreign privateers and by an increasing number of pirates. Many a Somerset vessel fell prey to one or the other. These various intruders prudently withdrew when the wounded pockets of Bristol merchants successfully persuaded the Navy Board to send a naval vessel, but they returned as soon as this deterrent was withdrawn and began to penetrate further and further up the channel. Not that our national record is much better in this respect, the Welsh especially being the subject of many indignant complaints.

As time moved on and excise duties rose to pay for government over-spending, the Bristol Channel experienced its fair share of smuggling. Many of the local populace were either involved or complicit and local seamen could not have been immune from temptation, especially with more than a few venal customs officers about. Despite all these negative factors the wider world was changing. The sixteenth century began an era of world exploration with its tremendous stimulus to trade. There followed the rise of the merchant class, together with all the facilities it required to make profits — warehousing, agents, credit, insurance and the like.

While, later, great Somerset enterprises like that of Stuckey & Bagehot might proudly operate East Indiamen out of Combwich and emigrants might sail from Bridgwater to North America, the pattern of Bristol activity was always the dominant feature in the profile of shipping within the Bristol Channel, at least until steam power and railways came to the South Wales coal mines. Shipments through Bristol did decline for a while when the West Country woollen industry diminished in importance from the fifteenth century, but the volume of Irish

Bristol was a dominant influence on local shipping activity and this view from the Clifton Suspension Bridge shows a typical scene with a tug towing two ketches and a smack, a dredging operation off the north bank and a number of small vessels further downstream.

trade grew, as did that to the Atlantic coast of Europe. The first half of the seventeenth century saw the beginning of a steady growth in Bristol's industrial activity and the use of large numbers of vessels to carry its products. By 1650 the trade with North America had equalled that to and from Ireland. Then came the era of slave trading and its ancillary barter activity, the slave ships working their sad course in a triangle out to West Africa, across to the Americas and home with the rich produce of the New World. It was displaced in turn by the growth in direct business with the West Indies, especially sugar, molasses and rum.

The Minehead and Bridgwater harbour groups were not greatly dissimilar in terms of volume of shipping. At the beginning of the eighteenth century the number of vessels recorded at Bridgwater usually exceeded the Minehead figure, but not always. The main flow into the Minehead group was that of coal and culm from Swansea and Neath; these and other traffics from Pembrokeshire and Carmarthen formed the second highest inwards total for the group as a whole, with those from Bristol and beyond the third. There was a similar inward pattern at Bridgwater, but with rather more manufactured and transhipped goods from Bristol and cargoes from harbours up the Severn.

Inward voyages to Minehead and Bridgwater, principally livestock plus coal and other minerals, usually exceeded 300 a year at this period, but outward movements would only be about a third of this total. This reflected the character of the areas around the two ports, with cereals, fodder crops and produce the main commodities dispatched, plus to a smaller extent, flax, hemp and linen. An immense variety of other goods requiring shipment were offered in very varied and irregular quantities and ranged from ale to cabbage plants and pit props to cereals.

In comparison, Bristol was served by some 1,500 local trade voyages a year, with Severn trows bringing in ironwork from the Wye works, produce from the Cotswolds in addition to the Somerset supplies, and meat, hides, linen and the like from Ireland. Market boats worked regularly to and from Chepstow, Caerleon and Newport and there was a weekly link with Bridgwater.

With large numbers of Welsh and Irish cattle being shipped to Somerset and landed pretty well anywhere required, this would have been a very common scene.

Inevitably, this broad picture of Somerset coastal trade prior to the great changes from the 1790s onwards is something of a generalisation. Account needs to be taken of the varying integrity of early records which, even in later years, depended on the location and efficiency of the various customs houses and of a rather mixed bag of harbour authorities. While cargoes of higher value needed underwriting and their dispatch and arrival recorded, small and low-value goods could be moved without security under Letpass and similar documentation. Customs officials were not greatly concerned with the latter, but even small vessels might take on high-value goods by transhipment which might, or might not, get noticed. Additionally, masters might act as merchants for a little trading of their own, a feature often involving small coal shipments from the Neath area pits from which half the output was going to Somerset in 1701–05, taking over from the former livestock pre-eminence. The small movements for friends, other seamen and the local entrepreneurs would also feature.

The trade patterns of the past began a dramatic revision as the nineteenth century approached. Land enclosure and new machinery totally changed agriculture. First turnpike roads and then canals revolutionised inland distribution, steam usurped the former water-power dependence, and shipping increased in importance as an economic bulk movement agency. Vessels were now to get bigger, their operation more sophisticated and navigation and harbour facilities quick to follow suit. A comprehensive postal service speeded up the process of matching loads with shipping and the arrangement of agencies, credit and the like. Primitive lighthouses like the 1737 privately-owned, coal-fired lighthouse on Flat Holm, which was reconstructed by Trinity House in 1820, came under that body's unified control and charts could now be relied upon.

The whole of national life, not just its coastal shipping, was to change dramatically under the influence of the Industrial Revolution, ubiquitous railways, expanding mines, new docks, urban housing and other such factors. Throughout, coal remained a dominant feature of shipping activity in the Bristol Channel. Around 1790 steam power was increasingly being used in the South Wales collieries, and Dean coal pits were producing 100,000 tons a year as the 1800s arrived. Helped by tramways and their link to Lydney from 1813 and stimulated by the repeal of duty measures in 1833, the annual Dean output had risen to over 500,000 tons by 1880 – some 60 per cent going to Bridgwater. The rise in shipment coal was even more dramatic at Cardiff and Newport, especially after the Taff Vale Railway established the first feeder route in 1840–41. Coastal shipping trade adapted from the former local produce and other traditional movements to cope with the new opportunities presented by the demand for coal along with parallel growth such as the dispatch of large volumes of bricks from the Parrett ports, stone outwards for docks and sea walls, the short-lived iron ore export boom at Watchet and similar flows. The wines, tea, spices and other long-distance imports also increased, but were now supplemented by more exotic luxury goods from further destinations, either landed from deep sea vessels or, more often, transhipped by them at Bristol.

The Somerset ports and pills were now entering their heyday. Most coastal communities had seamen living there, along with many others connected with the sea. A busy port like Bridgwater would be dominated by the talk and movement of waterborne goods and its vessels, by the carriers and merchants working in the docks and the lives and needs of the seamen. Prior to the opening of the Severn Tunnel in 1886 the port had dealt with over 4,000 vessels in the peak years and traded with the United States, Canada, Newfoundland, Prussia and Russia in addition to the many home and local ports. Some three-quarters of the sailings were inwards with significant quantities of timber, twine, hemp, linseed, grain and general goods being handled, as well as coal. Timber also moved in the other direction, along with cement, plaster of Paris, gypsum, building bricks, scouring bricks, pipes and tiles. The character of each harbour location and its role and activity had become more complex and more individual, as will become apparent in the later descriptions of the various Somerset ports and their trade.

Despite a gradual slowing down it so continued until the dawn of the twentieth century, but the writing was already on the wall. The number of vessels bringing cargo into Bridgwater, for example, had dropped by a quarter between 1890 and 1892, but between the dawn of the new century and the outbreak of the First World War the drop was nearer a half, although the average load had risen only from 55 tons to 66 tons. After the war the decline became dramatic with the port depending on coal for four-fifths of its inbound business and fertilisers, sand and gravel for most of the rest. Outward flows had virtually ceased altogether.

Steamers and motor vessels featured increasingly in the Somerset harbours in these later years, but the railways had won the battle for the homeland traffics. They made use of water shipment themselves by bringing coal and rails into Highbridge Wharf and serviced the shipping's trade distribution needs from Portishead, Bridgwater and Watchet, at least until the railway industry itself went on to face its own nemesis in the rise of road transport. Portishead Docks were busy for many years with timber, phosphorus and coal for the power stations there and a few small steamers supplied local gasworks at Minehead and Weston-super-Mare.

Even the Bristol Channel's excursion steamers eventually surrendered their record of pleasure voyages, but Combwich did have a useful period of handling construction traffic for the Hinkley Point nuclear power plant, a few sand boats continued to come up to Bristol and, against all the odds, modern coastal shipping found a new role in bringing in coal and stone to Dunball Wharf. At the other end of the size scale, by the dawn of this century a succession of huge car carrying and coal vessels were using the new docks at Portbury.

3. THE VESSELS

Over the centuries, vessels of innumerable different designs, rigs and purposes have sailed the waters off the Somerset coast, from Viking longboats and pirate galleys to sleek schooners, laden barques and brigs, from fishing smacks to East Indiamen, and from revenue cutters to men-of-war. Sail ruled until the later years of the nineteenth century with the volume of activity accelerating steadily from the Tudor years onwards to a peak in the mid 1800s, steam then gradually becoming more commonplace. There were huge leaps in trade volume and vessel numbers in times of war and industrial growth with slumps often following.

The classic range of sailing vessels had its origins in the first attempts to harness the extra propulsion wind could add to clumsy oars and paddles. A short mast and a square sail had the advantage of simplicity, in terms not only of handling, but also in the processes of stepping the mast and providing a strong but manageable sail. The lug sail, along with other variations, all had their day. However, although a square or similar sail might capture a steady wind, it had its shortcomings in tricky conditions of water and weather and was hardly the perfect instrument for easy ship handling and manoeuvrability. A fore and aft sail with a free boom was one answer, but experience over years of seamanship produced others and fed them back to the shipwrights and sailmakers. In parallel with the evolution of the sail marched the skill of the craftsmen in wood in selecting timbers and working and joining them to provide the extra length and stability needed to provide the platform on which more generous sails might be rigged.

A taller mainmast with a topsail above the mainsail would capture more wind, a factor at the heart of fast schooner design and of the famous maritime clipper breed. Upper topsails would harness even more wind and repeating the combination on further masts took it one stage further. Square sails alone had their drawbacks when sailing in confined or unpredictable waters and the remedy was to either mix in a fore and aft sail on the mainmast or just add another mast and provide it with a fore and aft sail. Such mizzen masts became commonplace and together the two types provided both speed and manoeuvrability.

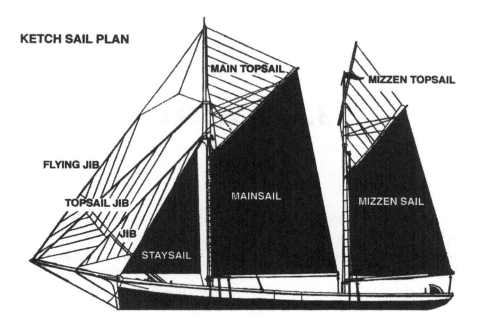

KETCH SAIL PLAN

MAIN TOPSAIL

MIZZEN TOPSAIL

FLYING JIB

TOPSAIL JIB

MAINSAIL

MIZZEN SAIL

JIB

STAYSAIL

Drawing showing the principal sails, in this case forming the rig of a typical ketch. (Roy Gallop)

Clearly the overall length of a vessel governed the number of masts it could accommodate, but it could be effectively lengthened for sail-bearing purposes by adding a bowsprit. Jib sails could then supplement a foresail and be anchored to the mainmast to prove a valuable addition to every aspect of a ship's performance. Inner, outer and flying jib sails became a feature of many commercial sailing vessels, sometimes as many as five. Happily, a long bowsprit extending from an upswept stem not only worked well in sailing terms, but could also emphasise the graceful, sea-friendly lines of a vessel's hull. Another useful add-on was achieved by providing gaffs to the principal masts and squeezing in a stay sail or two.

Any substantial alterations to the pattern of a vessel's sails clearly had consequences in terms of the size of crew needed to handle them, and thus on its operational costs. It would also affect how well, or badly, she handled, something not always foreseeable when the alterations were made. A new rig needed to be tested and changed if not producing the desired results. Nor was every alteration the outcome solely of thoughtful consideration. Cost and availability of materials were also major considerations and extra sails were frequently sourced from whatever happened to be handy. Many an old sail was acquired cheap and put to use, often after being cut to fit its new purpose. The best bits of a large sail might be perfectly suitable for a smaller role and the necessary cutting and stitching be well within the ability of a vessel's own crew.

Hulls followed a similar irregular pattern of development, but with a much simpler relationship between profile and use. In shallow waters a flat bottom was called for to allow for the grounding that was part of most voyages. Where the intended trade was not primarily between limited pills and harbours, a good beam not only increased cargo space but also provided stability when lying on the bottom to load or unload. Many estuaries developed their own peculiar vessel designs, but a common feature was a strong, solid construction able to withstand the regular knocks from wharves, rocks and other vessels and to survive a lesser grounding or listing incident. For deeper waters a deeper keel was needed for water 'purchase'.

There was, of course, another side to this progression. More masts and sails meant higher building and running costs and thus had to be justified by the trade on offer. Fitting out was costly too, with mounting expense for the rising volume and sophistication of running gear, tackle, ropes, sailcloth and the like. More seamen with better experience were also needed. Serious thought and sizeable pockets were all essentials of the business of shipbuilding, owning and operating.

Like all generalisations there were plenty of exceptions, chief among which was the fact that few ships remained in the same ownership for overlong. Start-up businesses would often buy a vessel second-hand and, just as often, make some alteration to its hull or rigging to suit whatever need they had in mind or just to reflect the experience and preferences of a new owner. A ship's history could well be a long and convoluted saga with names changed almost as frequently as ownership.

The overall picture in the Bristol Channel and the Severn Estuary was that of quite large numbers of sailing vessels with a dozen or so different types intent on their varying activities. With their size, sailing characteristics and handling methods equally varied, staying clear of one another and of navigational hazards was no mean undertaking. The scene at places like The Shoots or off the mouth of the Avon must have had something in common with a modern motorway junction except, of course, that the variety of 'vehicles' was infinitely greater, their power source was often highly unreliable and sudden braking was totally impossible!

The Sloop or Smack

The early years of channel trade, even more so than on the River Severn, were very much the province of simple sloops and smacks, single-masted and relying on mainsail and foresail to supplement the tide. Cutters, luggers and yawls were also to be seen, but the sloop was much favoured for its basic simplicity and versatility. Its simple rig, successor to that of the early fishing smacks, made for

The sloop rig was widely used by smaller
vessels; this arrangement was both
simple and effective. (Roy Gallop)

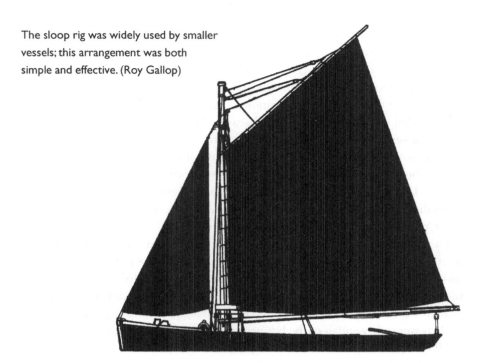

ease of handling, but did have its limitations. The forward location of the mast led
to a tendency to plunging in head-on heavy seas. Heaving-to was also difficult in
a sloop, and this was a decided disadvantage in the seas of the upper channel and
Severn Estuary with their small and tricky harbours. In its cutter form some of
the sloop's drawbacks were alleviated.

The Cutter

Larger than the sloop, the cutter's fore and aft rig of mainsail and two foresails
created a fast, handy vessel, especially efficient in windward sailing. Their use for
cargo was limited, but the channel waters would at one time have revealed a great
many cutters, mainly as pilot boats roaming out as far as Lundy to meet incoming
merchantmen. Sturdily built, with a deep draught and wide beam derived from
this activity, their 40–60ft length also gave them room for the boarding punt, a
decent cabin and adequate space for all the gear and provisions. Pilot cutters could
lie to in heavy seas when waiting, a frequent occurrence in the days when sailing
and voyage times for deep-sea shipping were totally dependent on weather and
the pattern of incoming merchantmen unpredictable. The waiting time would
be spent fishing, but the cutter could then produce speed and manoeuvrability
when required, an important feature when seeking to board an incoming vessel

before the opposition could make its bid. And yet these handy little craft were still within the capacity of a man and a boy, and of the latter to bring home on his own after the pilot had left.

Happily, the type still survives as revealed in a later chapter.

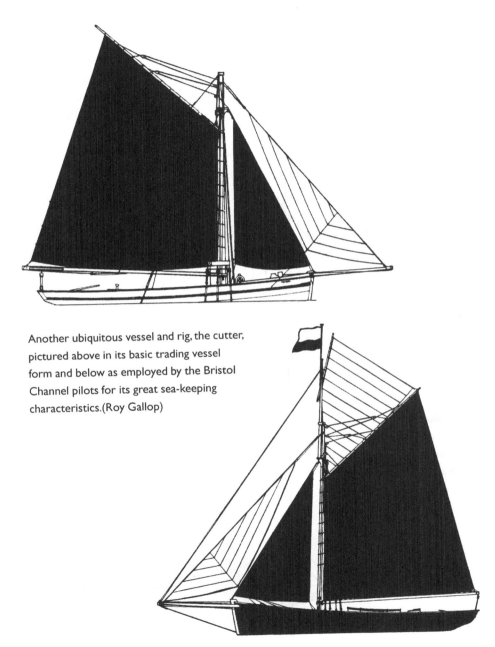

Another ubiquitous vessel and rig, the cutter, pictured above in its basic trading vessel form and below as employed by the Bristol Channel pilots for its great sea-keeping characteristics. (Roy Gallop)

The Trow

The Severn trow was first cousin to the Humber keel and, like the latter, was a very simple vessel, originally just a straightforward shallow-draught barge with bluff bow, open hold and square stern. Working upstream from Gloucester necessitated a pivoted mast, pinned in a simple box so that it could easily be lowered towards the stern to negotiate bridges, and just as easily raised again. The mast also served to anchor the towing rope and facilitate loading and unloading. For their work along the length of the Upper and Middle Severn the single mast and square sail were adequate to supplement the tides as far as these reached, and towing was the practice beyond. Water depths were critical on the Severn, hence the shallow draught and flat bottom. Progress could even be influenced by the

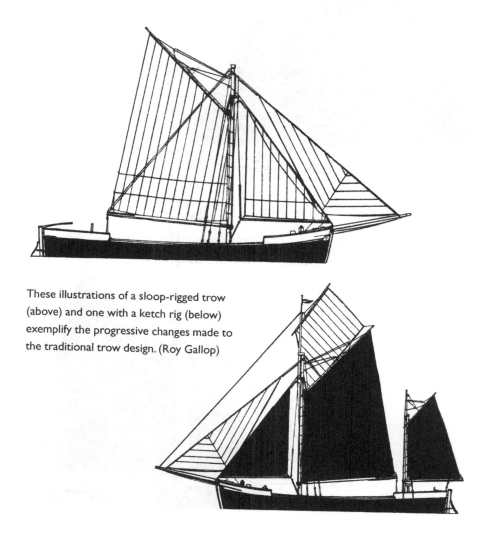

These illustrations of a sloop-rigged trow (above) and one with a ketch rig (below) exemplify the progressive changes made to the traditional trow design. (Roy Gallop)

amount of rain coming down from the Welsh hills where the Severn rose, and result in small fleets coming down river together. The vessels waiting to go up river could then take similar advantage of the additional water depth.

The trow dates back at least to the fifteenth century and its original homelands were the waters above Gloucester and those of the River Wye. There the square rig persisted for a good 400 years, but changes in the trow's environment from around 1830 forced change upon traders, traffic patterns and upon the vessels and their owners and crews. Steam was the agent of a massive alteration, first in the form of the availability of steam towage and then in the growth in railway companies and their networks – the Taff Vale 1840, South Wales Railway 1850, Severn Bridge 1879 and Severn Tunnel 1886. The whole pattern of transport altered and this simple vessel had to alter to reflect this. It had to work further afield, increase its load and speed up its turnaround if it was to stay in business. From the middle of the century the traditional trow profile was giving way to a much bigger craft suitable for more open waters.

Not only did vessels need to become bigger and capable of carrying a better payload but seaworthiness now became a major consideration. The Severn was always tricky because of its varying depths, but once in the Bristol Channel there was always a prospect of severe storms and other hazards. The combination of an open hold and low freeboard was now an invitation to trouble, especially damage to cargo or even swamping. The traditional side cloths were no protection against bad channel weather and many of the trows facing change had the sides and ends of the hold built up while others, the box trows, had side decks and coamings added. Tarpaulins as the standard form of cargo protection gave way to conventional hatch boards.

Many trows were given a mizzen mast and a bowsprit, and some were lengthened by the insertion of a section amidships. With the ability to add various foresail and topsail extras they became ketch-rigged and capable of regular journeys as far as Porlock and Barry or even further, while remaining within the manning capacity of two crewmen or two men and a boy. The new breed of larger vessels could take on a heavy load from the coal chutes at Lydney, Newport, Cardiff, Barry, Neath and Swansea and worked well beyond the former Somerset destinations.

The traditional trow had an oak frame and deep, strong beech keelson, the inside keel which added longitudinal strength. The bottom strakes were of 3in elm and the planking of 3in pitch pine. At one time 20 tons would be a good load, but later overall dimensions ranged up to 70ft in length and loading capability of up to 100 tons or more. Hull profiles changed less than other aspects although some slight rounding took place, albeit without sacrificing the essential flat bottom. Most of the new breed of vessels retained the age-old, near-flat bottom hull, but might have a deeper keel or manage with a detachable keel which had to

The sad end of the life of a trow, the *Severn Trader*, pictured at Purton in 2003 and still revealing much of the construction of her upper works, including the rather plain traditional transom. Some of the vessel's alterations are clear, including the housing for an auxiliary engine. (Roy Gallop)

be floated into position and secured with chains. A high keelson provided added strength and an aid to dividing and so balancing the coal loads.

These later vessels would typically be of some 6ft draught, 17ft wide and be decked forward (for stores) and aft (for living accommodation). Protection against swell might now come not only from the traditional side cloths or sideboards but, in many cases, from higher bulwarks and hatch covers. The combination of extra sail and larger holds enabled this new generation of ketch-rigged trows to operate effectively in their new and larger environment of the Bristol Channel proper.

The Ketch

The most popular rig of all from around 1870 onwards, that of a two-part foremast and shorter mizzen, was carried by that most ubiquitous of the channel trading vessels, the ketch. Early vessels with this rig were often converted smacks or sloops with the ketch ranks later being joined by many former trows and even by schooners, all pressurised into the simplest effective rig by low freight rates and the constraints of weather and by the need for high utilisation, all of which contributed to making cutting crew costs imperative. As trows were converted to the two-masted fore-and-aft ketch rig, this format came to dominate, especially as a ketch could point higher into the wind and cope better with the wind variations of coastal waters.

The most favoured rig, versatile and easy for a small crew to handle, the ketch was the mainstay of the Bristol Channel trade for many years. (Roy Gallop)

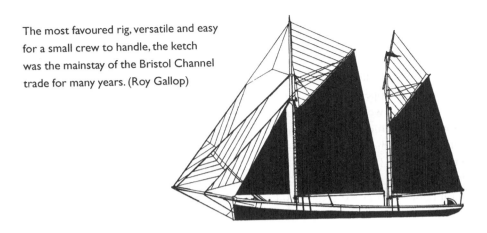

New-built ketches had more pretensions to looks than the traditional trows, with a better shape based on a carvel-built hull with a somewhat less flat bottom, a counter stern in place of the former vertical transom and with much sweeter lines at the bow. To the basic rear mizzen mast and the mainmast forward, a topsail was sometimes added above the mainsail gaff, while a bowsprit permitted jib sails in front of the foresail, something which proved handy when going to windward. This extra provision gave the ketch better balance, speed and handling qualities and, unlike many trows, they were normally provided with an overall hatch cover. Yawls, although similar apart from the siting of the mizzen mast aft of the rudder post, were less common in local waters. The ketch rig could be tricky in windward sailing, but was still near ideal for the waters in which it worked.

A classic scene with a ketch, the most ubiquitous of local sailing vessels, at anchor in Minehead Harbour, probably awaiting its next cargo.

The Schooner

Schooners also appeared in local harbours. Built for speed and manoeuvrability by having fore and aft sails with various additions – square sails, foresails, topsails, gaff sails – they naturally needed more handling and incurred manning costs extra to the standard skipper, mate and, possibly, boy crew of the simpler trows and ketches. This had to be weighed against how much more could be carried with the faster transit times achievable. Performance to windward could be poor, but quite the opposite with the wind on or abaft the beam. Schooners were versatile in sailing terms and could cope well with bad weather as the largest sail was amidships and the mainsail could be stowed in favour of a trysail on the mainmast.

Of course, not every vessel fitted neatly into the basic categories of sailing rig. Compared with a steamer, a sailing vessel was not so costly as to be completely beyond the aspirations of ordinary seafarers, and a large proportion had a single owner, albeit in the form of several investors. This led to a great deal of individuality for one thing and, for another, the choice of vessel for a new owner or owners was frequently dictated by the limitation on funds. If a new build could not be afforded, frequently the case, the vessel acquired depended on what happened to be on the market at the time, and second-hand purchases were more likely to vary a lot in condition. They would also reflect the previous owner's preference for rigging and the extent to which he had been able to maintain

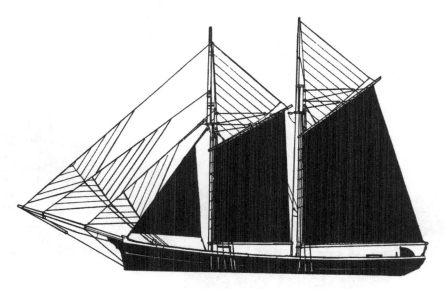

This schooner rig had many similarities to that of a ketch except that the mainmast was towards the stern of the vessel. It was mostly used on bigger vessels but, because of the larger sail area, more hands were needed. Ketches tended to be more manageable, but the schooner had the edge in speed. (Roy Gallop)

his charge. Little was standard or permanent in the sphere of sailing vessel rigs, condition, appearance or performance.

Even when a new master, and any backers he had, started up in business, few would make such generous profits as to be able to keep their vessel immaculate at all times. Seaworthiness was always the prime consideration, but 'make do

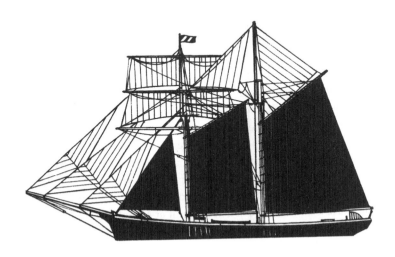

Two schooner variations, one (above) with square topsails to increase canvas area and produce extra speed and the other (below) where having three smaller, common sails eased the work of handling them. Rare visitors to Somerset harbours, such vessels would frequently be encountered in the Bristol Channel along with barques, brigs and, later, steamers. (Roy Gallop)

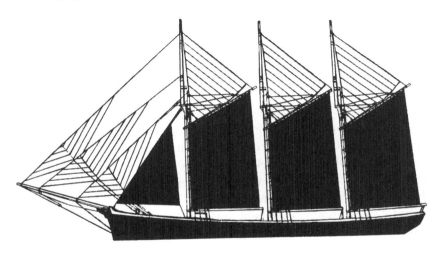

and mend' was a very real concept. A torn sail had to be mended or patched, a broken mast might have to be shortened or abandoned, a new spar crudely shaped from timber that could be found, scrounged or purloined. Important though they were, few ropes would have been in pristine condition. Splicing was an essential skill for seamen.

At its peak the sailing vessel activity in the Bristol Channel and Severn Estuary would have been a glorious mixture of every type of vessel imaginable and each likely to display the character of its owners, its trade and its circumstances.

Building

In the heyday of sail in the waters of the Severn and the Bristol Channel, at any one time about half of the working vessels would have been built in the area they served. The rest were of motley origins, emanating from southern English ports, Scotland, Europe, and even further afield.

The principal boat building activity of the area was centred on Ilfracombe, on the Barnstaple/Bideford estuarial waters, at Bridgwater and Bristol and on the river and canals in and around Gloucester. Bridgwater had several boatyards as well as dry dock facilities and produced around 140 vessels in the nineteenth century while quite a few small vessels were built at Minehead. Fairly large vessels could be and were built at Chepstow and smaller ones were completed from time to time at Lydney and Redbrook.

Building took place at Gloucester itself, but was significantly exceeded by the group of yards at Saul, which built ships up to 75 tons, and at Brimscombe, Framilode and Stroud. In the earlier years the majority of vessels from this area at least started their lives as a trow and might draw as little as 3ft to recognise the shallow waters of their canal and Severn homeland. Because of its location there was also a great deal of building for the canal network and of barges for horse or tug towage.

In addition to the main Somerset building yards capable of constructing sizeable vessels, irregular building of smacks and other smaller vessels took place at Porlock Weir and other small harbours, even on the beach with a launch on rollers on completion. Building was also carried on at several inland locations, including Langport where a 66-ton ketch was built around 1847 for fitting out at Bridgwater, and the odd small, one-off craft could originate from quite small places such as Bleadon. An ongoing business in repairs and conversions beyond the capacity or ingenuity of the crew was another feature of almost all these places and some would have a vessel on the stocks as work in hand, to be pushed forward when time and money permitted. Generally speaking, the smaller the port the smaller the vessels that were built there.

The Bristol shipyards were quite well equipped, but most Somerset enterprises were only modest in size. Certainly in the early years they had no elaborate

Although the location of his inspiration is not known, the artist has conveyed an excellent idea of the near-universal method of building wooden vessels other than in a dry dock. (Dover Publications)

facilities and no complicated tools. What they did have was an understanding of timber and where to obtain wood of the right type and shape, and the know-how then to use it successfully. The location might be no more than a flat surface with water access, possibly in the form of a shallow hollow into which water could be admitted to aid the launching process (although small hulls were even launched over the quay wall occasionally at some places). From that point onward the essentials were a firm foundation for the keel and the timbers to prop the vessel upright as work on the hull progressed. Lifting would be done by sheer legs, shaping by traditional tools and fixing by joints, nails and plugs.

The same essentials applied at Bridgwater, at least until cranes and powered saws came along. There, the development of the port in the nineteenth century resulted in increasing shipbuilding activity. Axford & Son are recorded as building the 800-ton barque *Pathfinder* which was launched to great acclaim in 1852 and made a maiden voyage from the port to New York. On the West Quay, the Crowpill Shipbuilding Yard launched a vessel named after local naval hero

Admiral Blake five years later. She was a smaller vessel of 190 tons and just 100ft long. In 1864 John Gough's business as shipbuilders and repairers added the 400-ton *Cesarea* to the Bridgwater tally. The final addition to a long and honourable list was that of the 99-ton ketch *Irene* which came from the yard of F.J. Carver & Sons in 1907 to take up a life of carrying local bricks for her owners Colthurst Symons & Co. Ltd. Carvers owned Bridgwater's dry dock at the downstream end of East Quay, just beyond the port's well-used gridiron. This latter structure was an essential dock feature, allowing vessels to be settled on its raised, cross-timbered base at high tide so that attention could be given to the area of the hull exposed when the water level was lower. Many a bruised timber or leaking seam was put right on the gridiron.

Most shipbuilders, and especially the smaller concerns, depended for their livelihood more on repairs than on new building. This source of work continued for a time after the building of wooden ships ended with the dawn of the twentieth century, but as vessels became too old for economic service this work dried up as well, and with it the shore facilities to keep the surviving vessels earning. If a repair was beyond the competence of its crew or a local carpenter, one more hull had to be sold for scrap, burned or left to rot. Very few shipbuilders made the change from wood to steel construction, certainly not the small ones.

The equipment of the wooden shipbuilders, both large and small, was very unsophisticated by today's standards of power tools and computer-controlled machinery. On a simple site, often without the basic protection of even a home-made wooden shed, the shipbuilder practised his art in the design of the vessel, the selection of timbers for its construction and the process of measuring, shaping and fitting them into the required pattern. A 'feel' for the wood and 'an eye' for shape and measurement were essentials.

Local timber was used if suitable in type and shape, often purchased on site after inspection. Oak and elm could be had from the Forest of Dean if none was available locally. A sawpit was the first step after selection with final shaping as keel, frames, knees, bracket and planks achieved with the adze, heating taking place as necessary for bending. Discarded timber would be stored in a pile for possible later use and a store of props had always to be on hand. A grindstone, vices, windlass and simple jacks would all be needed and yards always had a motley array of paints and the smaller tools like augers, hammers and so on.

The majority of vessels owned and operated out of Somerset's harbours had a chequered pedigree, passing from one owner to another as circumstances dictated and frequently subject to changes to hull, sails or other features in the process. A three-part division of net earnings was common, albeit only one of several similar business norms, with one part to the owner or owners, one for the vessel's upkeep and one for the master and crew. The latter thus had a vested interest in their vessel's equipment, handling and ability to earn a decent living, in addition to the basic instinct for self-preservation. The builder might be a part-owner or have agreed to accept some deferred payments from the vessel's earnings in which case his interest did not end with its move from yard to sea.

Not unusual in the varied life of many sailing vessels was the *Jane*. Her 140-year life had begun at Runcorn in 1800 and over her lifetime she had changed rigs in stages from sloop to ketch. In this form, 62ft long, with a flush deck and capable of carrying 80 tons she was owned at Uphill by Captain Smart and a local coal merchant. Like many others of her kind *Jane* finished her working life as a Bristol lighter and was broken up around 1940.

While there was no fixed pattern, of course, those vessels not dedicated to a particular owner or trade were subject to a sort of downgrading, a phenomenon which today would be labelled 'cascading'. A good example was the *Flying Foam* of Bridgwater, a twin-mast, 100-ton topsail schooner which had been built in Jersey in 1879. After a period of ocean-going in the Newfoundland trade, she cut back her activities to the Welsh slate business. Then, like many others of her kind, she entered a sort of twilight as a regular carrier of china clay from the Fowey Estuary. Both the slate traffic and the china clay were available in quantity and attracted many vessels seeking a cargo. *Flying Foam* survived the setback of sitting on her anchor in 1931, but sank five years later en route from Liverpool to Plymouth with coal. In other ships' careers, coal from the Bristol Channel to Ireland and salt from Runcorn would have featured regularly.

Whatever the vessel, the aim was always regular business over the shortest possible route with maximum use of the tide, sometimes even an out and home journey in one cycle. This driving factor limited the attention paid by boatbuilders and owners to the comfort and well-being of the crew. Living and working conditions were spartan, calling for a skilled and hardy breed of men who might make a reasonable living in the good weather months, but had to be ready to find other loads or other jobs in the bad times. They were not expected to have much non-working time while at sea or handling cargoes. Thus on board accommodation provided for the crew would be limited to the aft cabin and this would consist of little more than rough bunks, table, shelves and the essential stove. Space for crew and equipment became even scarcer when marine engines usurped the rear cabin space, another conversion job for the builders.

Inland

Less notable, but equally diverse, was the range of smaller vessels used in coastal and inland waters. Small sailing and rowing boats of several designs served countless fishermen in the inshore waters and estuaries and rowing dinghies operated around all the harbours, the larger ones accommodating several oarsmen to undertake towage of sea-going vessels. The trading vessels themselves all had their own small boat while others were in constant use by pilots, chandlers, merchants, port and drainage officials, customs men and others going about their day-to-day business of supply, trade and inspection.

In the earlier years, small smacks carrying coal, culm and other commodities not only used the coastal harbours but penetrated surprising distances up rivers and creeks. Barges and canal narrowboats took over where they left off and, increasingly as the waterways were steadily improved, penetrated well inland, reaching beyond Taunton, up to Ilchester and Westport, even quite near to Cheddar. Some commodities were transferred from sea-going vessel to barge at Combwich for their onward journey along the Parrett. In other cases this transhipment took place at Bridgwater to the extent that, even before improvement of the Parrett route, the volume of business moving along the river to and from Langport and beyond was around 50,000 tons annually. The

This type of barge would have been a common sight on the River Parrett before the coming of the railway. While coal was the main upriver traffic, small cargoes of other goods would often have been added. (Roy Gallop)

barges used were of traditional design and had a carrying capacity of 15–20 tons. The restrictive bridge at Langport meant transhipment to smaller barges, of 5–7½ tons for movement beyond. The business on the Tone (and subsequently the Bridgwater & Taunton Canal), especially coal to Ham Mills, was equally significant. One variation in the general barge pattern was the tub boats of the Chard Canal.

Simple shallow-draught, low freeboard and wide, stable workboats were numerous in the Somerset Levels where narrow rhynes abounded, flooding was commonplace and road access was not always practicable. Their principal role was in the carriage of willows or of peat turves, but they were used for whatever was required, visiting market, moving goods and machinery, supplying fodder to livestock and being, in effect, completely general purpose. Most farms and growers had at least one and, until the advances in drainage and road construction, life would have been near-impossible without these water workhorses. Their simple design also meant that they could be constructed by local craftsmen, perhaps just the village carpenter.

The willow-carrying boats were the larger of the two types, anything up to 20ft in length, and usually about 6ft in the beam. The five oak planks used for the flat bottom at the centre tapered to one or two at each end, giving the boat a double bow which made it easy for moving through water vegetation and also had the big advantage of being capable of use without being turned. The low sides would be of elm, tar would be applied inside and out and the finished vessel was punted, towed or propelled with a single oar from the rear. A flat bottom permitted maximum versatility and the stability to be loaded high with the harvested willows. Most had two-plank sides which were secured to the bottom boards with inverted 'knees'.

The boats used for turf, or peat, were similar to those which carried willows, but mostly slightly smaller and with a gunwale surmounting the elm plank sides. All these boats could be laden to a surprising height with a load of up to half a ton, and their versatility was not only proven but a matter of some pride. They would 'float on dew', it was frequently said.

The mixture of barges, narrowboats and overgrown flatners which carried the trade cargoes inherited a water movement tradition that dated back to the days of Glastonbury Abbey and waterways like the Pilrow Cut. In those times supplies for the abbey were carried by water and its officials used smaller boats to move around the abbey properties arranging, communicating, inspecting and conducting other abbey business.

Barges engaged in inland trade used the tide where it ran and were towed elsewhere. Stables existed at the junction of the Parrett and Tone rivers to supply the horses needed for towage beyond the tidal limit on these rivers, and a number of boatmen also lived in the area. Stuckey & Bagehot had a large fleet, other

In versions of different length, these flatners performed many varied tasks on the waterways of the Somerset Levels. Although mainly used to carry willows or peat, they would also be used for coal, manure and a variety of other goods to and from isolated places. (Roy Gallop)

concerns owned several barges and quite a few were 'owner-operated'. Canal companies were also barge owners, both for trading and for maintenance activity, the Bridgwater & Taunton Canal having at least two sizeable vessels of its own.

But trading vessels were not the only users of the waterways. It is clear from the reports of the opening of the Glastonbury Canal in 1833 that some private vessels were also in existence. The canal company's own barge *Goodland* played a leading role in the ceremonial opening voyages and was partnered by a 'beautiful yacht', the *Water Witch*. A new yacht, the *St Vincent*, took part in a second celebration, but ran into trouble when she sprang a leak and the guests on board had to be rescued.

While the number of vessels without power was always far greater than those with engines of some sort, the wider rivers did lend themselves to the application of marine power when it became available. Towage was a prime area of opportunity with its potential for massive time savings. Keeping them clear of silt and weeds was another.

Silt was a constant problem for river and harbour authorities. Along the inland rivers it was the responsibility of the drainage authorities to control both silting and weeds. For centuries this had been the task of riverside landowners, but few saw it as their prime consideration and even when formal drainage authorities were established they had great problems in collecting the rates levied. The position slowly improved, but still based on the traditional use of workboats with rakes and cutting tools, later supplemented by bucket grabs.

Its length and use made the River Parrett a big challenge in this respect and prompted a search for something more efficient. A grab vessel was tried but sank and the commissioners eventually approved a scheme by Bridgwater engineer Frank Wills for an 'eroder' vessel. A three-year contract heralded the twenty-three-year career of *Pioneer*, a shallow-draught, low-profile steam vessel based on a 35ft steel barge and fitted with a compound steam engine for propulsion and for powering the jets which flushed silt from the banks and channels. Where this accumulated in quantity the vessel could be held in position by stern ropes fixed to either bank and the long jet focussed on the offending area, agitating the silt for flushing away with the outgoing stream. *Pioneer* was at work until 1917.

Bridgwater Town Council was responsible, through its Port & Navigation Committee, for the lower Parrett reaches where maintaining port access was highly important to the shipping trade but, at the same time, the Bath Brick manufacturers were fiercely protective of their slime batches near the town. After much debate the committee decided to acquire its own eroder, eventually obtaining the 58ft *Eroder* from the Wills company. She was a similar vessel to *Pioneer*, but considerably longer. Working on the river between the town and the sea the new vessel was not without its problems if the harbour master's records are anything to go by. He penned many reports of poor steaming due to the use of low quality coal which also built up clinker on the fire bars and resulted in the loss of availability for clearance work. Quite a few other problems featured in the Bridgwater harbour master's reports in the later years, not least the Great Western Railway's habit of leaving chains lying about the quays.

One more eroder was still to come, in the shape of the 50ft *Perseverance*. Again from the Wills firm, she had three-cylinder Petter marine engines for propulsion and powering the six high-pressure water jets. *Perseverance* started work in 1933 and did her job well until made redundant by the post-war decline in Bridgwater shipping. She then worked as a combined silt remover and workboat at Watchet until the same fate overtook her there.

The benefits of mechanisation were even more apparent in the advent of steam towage. A group of Bridgwater and Langport shipping interests saw this and ordered their first tug, *Endeavour*, which was built in 1837. This could tow several large vessels upriver at one time and, coupled with the 1841 opening of the new dock, brought about a new era in the life of Bridgwater as a port. Not only was dependence on the tides greatly reduced, with a huge saving of the time spent waiting, but the services of the towing boats were no longer required and the need for transhipment at Combwich reduced. A second tug, *Perseverance*, was ordered in 1840. The two, and later vessels like the *Petrel* and *Victor*, were of quite simple design and were not above undertaking other jobs, including the occasional passenger excursion.

A notable non-coastal vessel was the drag boat used to clear silt in Bridgwater Dock. Believed to have been designed by Brunel for the Great Western Railway on the same pattern as one used in Bristol's floating harbour, this vessel was always known as *Bertha*. She was fabricated in Bristol around 1844 and assembled at

The drag boat known as *Bertha* moored in the inner dock at Bridgwater in 1968.

Bridgwater to produce a functional rectangular hull of riveted puddle iron plates with timber superstructure and a tall funnel. A single-cylinder, double-acting steam engine working at 40psi powered a cross-mounted shaft with flywheel, chain drum and winch. The 50-ton vessel had a scraper blade at the stern which could be lowered to allow silt to be scraped into underwater heaps by attaching a heavy chain to the dock bollards and then winding it in. The chain was then moved to the adjoining bollards and a lighter chain was used to return with the scraper raised so that the whole process could be repeated on an adjoining, parallel or semi-diagonal course. After scraping the mud into the outer basin, sluices were opened to let in water to swirl the unwanted sediment into the centre before side culverts carried it away into the main stream. *Bertha* survived the dock closure and, after a period on display at Exeter, is currently under restoration at Eyemouth.

The *Rexford* at Highbridge was not only used for dragging the mud away from the wharf for clearance by the tide, but also acted as tug and general purpose workboat. This essentially local vessel, owned by a local ex-navy man A.E. Buncombe, survived until the scrapyard claimed it around 1950, but not before she had brought in Highbridge's last visitor, the *Phoenix*. Watchet harbour's silt clearance and workboat lasted even longer.

4. ALL IN A DAY'S WORK

Today the waters of the Bristol Channel are frequently empty of any shipping whatsoever. A few small private fishing and leisure craft appear, mainly at holiday times when they are joined by the surviving excursion vessels, MV *Balmoral* and PS *Waverley*. The MV *Oldenberg* occasionally strays from her routine of serving Lundy Island and the veteran MV *Bristol Queen* enjoys another chapter in a long career by providing summer sailings from Knightstone Harbour at Weston-super-Mare. The trading ships are represented by the intermittent but ongoing procession of small coasters and other freighters bound for Sharpness, a container ship heading for Newport or one of the huge coal, ore or car carriers taking on their tugs for entry to Portbury Docks. The latter group are ugly, functional monsters, heavily pregnant with hundreds of cars, shrinking Flat Holm Island in their passing and they would make an unbelievable contrast with the graceful ketches that once roamed the same waters. The replica *Mathew* has made the odd appearance and there are occasional unusual visitors like heavy lift or naval vessels, even the occasional full-rigged sailing craft.

What a different scene it would have been in the past, especially in the nineteenth century. The wind, tide and weather were still the gods and waiting upon their pleasure a focal part of practical sailing. As a consequence huge numbers of vessels might be seen anchored in the regular spots in King Road, in the deeper channels off Cardiff and near Stert Island, and might total anything from ten to sixty vessels, all forced to wait until the conditions were right. And the mixture would contain smacks, sloops, luggers, trows, ketches, schooners and hybrids, all revealing a variety of shapes and rigs depending on their builders, skippers and trades. The variety in cargoes meant vessels sat in the water in different ways and their depth needs would determine when they could take the flowing tide upriver.

Before the godsend of the marine engine, sailing in the waters of the Severn Estuary and Bristol Channel required a very daunting mixture of skills. Any cargo sailing was invariably physically hard. It also demanded a feel for the effects of varying tide, wind and water flow and depth conditions which would vary from vessel to vessel depending on the hull profile, the load, the rig and each craft's idiosyncrasies. Depths, rocks, tide races, shoals, whirlpools and landmarks were another lesson, along with the nature of differing cargoes and the peculiarities of each individual harbour. Weather, running repairs, the management of the ship's rowing boat, handling the sails, winch, anchor and ropes and other gear – the list of skills to be mastered goes on. And not forgetting that essential ability to fry something appetising and make hot, strong, sweet tea. All skills traditionally handed down among families and picked up in the hard classroom of earning a living.

Traditionally crew members tended to be followers in their father's footsteps but, as commerce expanded, new seamen might be drawn from the land, from the fishing community, from shrinking trades and even from the workhouse. Crews did not live on board unless forced to do so by their sailings, and the homes of

Loading and unloading vessels in the main harbours was well organised, but in isolated coastal locations the scene would have been more like this. (Dover Publications)

the majority were in or near their home port. A crew would normally comprise skipper, mate and, possibly, a boy learning the trade, but larger vessels would often need the addition of a deckhand. Home life was hardly 'normal' for the hours were uncertain, the earnings unpredictable and the risk of injury, or even death, always present.

The channel trading activity was largely the province of single vessel owners but some traders like Ridler at Minehead and some of the larger manufacturing activities such as the Bridgwater brickworks either owned several vessels or controlled fleets they had contracted. Vessel ownership involved the costs of covering the original construction of the vessel and a return on that outlay, plus another group of costs associated with maintenance, e.g. sails, ropes and other chandlery items, also hull and cargo insurance, and then the actual costs incurred in carrying out a voyage. The latter would consist of payments for provisions, towage, harbour dues, trimming assistance and so on plus, of course, wages for the crew. Their earnings were in line with their status and responsibilities, those of the mate, for example, being generally slightly above the going rate of payment to an agricultural labourer. This difference between these two areas of employment widened steadily in favour of seamen and, even in their case, there were many variations between different owners and trades.

Vessel ownership might actually be part-ownership and involve as many as eighty shares. Those involved could range from farmers to tradesmen and often included shipbuilders who were willing to accept deferred payments to be made out of voyage earnings. Working vessels would have to carry some sort of cash float for paying dues, replenishing supplies and underwriting such contingencies as becoming windbound in some distant harbour, yet still having to eat. In some cases captains might also want to do a bit of trading on their own account and purchase a load of coal if it were offered cheap and could be sold for a profit. There is evidence that other transactions took place involving small extra cargoes and discreet payments, especially in the days before the revenue watchmen became well organised. An occasional 'passenger' might also be taken to visit a relative or to offer home-produced goods at some destination. Local migration among the families of seamen was quite commonplace.

Like the vessels employed in these waters, the actual freight movement varied greatly depending on the nature and size of the cargoes. Some vessels were owned by, contracted to or worked solely for one industry, e.g. bricks from Bridgwater and Combwich, and cement from Dunball. Many worked regularly on the same run, e.g. coal from Lydney, Newport, Cardiff and Swansea. Others carried any load they could get. Work that did not come directly from owners or a contract would usually be at the behest of an agent, but there was a lot of casual, short-term work and captains with no next load might try their luck anywhere that experience or rumour suggested one might be available.

Freight rates were a matter for negotiation and, for what would now be called 'jobbing', would depend on a cargo's nature, value and urgency and the degree of availability of vessels willing and able to carry it. No vessel wanted to sail empty and if getting an onward load meant trimming the rate, so be it. If the next load meant moving to another loading point, then the shorter the journey the better. The question of ballast also arose. Any vessel sailing empty in the Western Approaches or the Irish Sea, or in very bad weather, needed ballast to keep it low in the water and more stable, but not only was this a profitless cargo, suitable ballast had to be found, loaded and then removed before the next load. It might be anything from old metal to rocks, sand or rubble, but was to be avoided if any safe alternative was available. Occasionally, material suitable for ballast use might be purchased cheap and then sold at the next port of call. Ballast was also a sore subject for the harbour master at Bridgwater who was constantly complaining of it lying about on his wharves.

The early dependence on the post made the pre-planning of journeys difficult, and the advent of the telegraph system, eventually taken over by the Post Office, was a major development in freight shipping arrangements. Even so bad weather, crowded berths and other such difficulties could ruin arrangements, although it helped if the planned cargo came from or was intended for a warehouse, store or stack. Getting a profitable load factor depended heavily on agents and factors and on those harbours with a constant output or intake. Even then it could result in a voyage with as many as seven or eight different 'legs'.

The distance factor became even more important when a vessel was far from home, like the Colthurst Symons schooner which had taken a load of bricks to the North East and then got stranded on the French shore by rough weather on the way home. She was eventually just left there, along with her cargo of coals from Newcastle.

Bridgwater coal merchants like Sully & Co. would arrange their requirements with the colliery factor and engage a vessel to bring the traffic from the port of origin and would then, after arrival, send it on by rail or have it discharged to stack for local sale. Small coal merchants, often farmers as well, would do the same in a smaller way and hawk the coal around local villages by horse and cart. Early in the nineteenth century, for example, Parson Holland of Over Stowey sent his man to Combwich when he heard a coal boat had arrived, to bring back a load of coal for the parsonage.

Prior to the nineteenth century sailings were much less structured. The better weather season produced an increase in produce to be moved to the big city markets, but coal for industries and culm for kilns remained a constant need. Some seamen turned to farming or fishing in the winter or other slack periods, others had to weather the days when jobs were not available or sailing was impossible, perhaps turning to casual fishing as the short-term standby most

allied to their trade. There were occasions when the freezing of the River Parrett stopped all Bridgwater sailings for so long that seamen were forced to beg in the streets of the town. Vessel repairs and maintenance arrears could also be attended to during the winter months.

Shipping aids and regulations as we know them today were unheard of in the earlier sailing vessel times. Movement was a daytime activity whenever that was possible, and navigation lights a relatively modern feature, although a masthead anchor light was used during an overnight wait. Not that it would have shone very far! Light regulations date from 1858 and initially required a single lantern at bowsprit or masthead.

A suitable wind and tide combination was critical, as was an adequate depth of water. The tide pattern and variations – high and low, ebb and flow, neap, spring and flood – were known, wind and weather were a matter of experience, and observation and water depths were part of the sailor's essential knowledge. But there needed to be a constant check during every voyage against known bank or shore markers.

For a small trow with just a square sail making a trip depended totally on an assessment of when the tide would serve for getting away from the harbour and carrying the boat to its destination, assisted as necessary by a bit of sail use, warping or towing. It would require catching the ebb to emerge from the Parrett River and then a tangent course to use the incoming flood to move up-channel. Use of the sail would, given the right wind, make the process faster or paying for a tow might increase the permutations, but even with an engine a loaded vessel could make no headway against a typical 7 knot tide. Steerage way was essential, but might be hard to manage on a fast flood without some constant, sensitive and intuitive work on the rudder.

Navigation, or pilotage as it was referred to in coastal waters, was not sophisticated and would rarely involve more instruments than a lead line for the vital task of monitoring depths, and a compass, and sometimes not even a compass. Knowledge was the key, that vital understanding of the hazards of rocks, headlands, shoals and tide races and awareness of the various hills, church towers and other landmarks which would help a skipper to stay on a rough course. Seamen needed the ability to read the weather both early and when change was on the way and to know where to look for a sheltered anchorage if needed, for the ever-present element of waiting out a storm or for the tide to turn.

Opposite: Inwards cargo at proper wharves would be unloaded to quay for outside stacking or warehouse storage and would eventually need horse transport to get to its final destination. (Dover Publications)

Other, more subtle, skills derived from sheer experience, e.g. how to read the sound from the sails or those of water passing beneath the hull, the idiosyncrasies of harbours and other vessels and an eye for changes in trim, the sluggishness of too much water in the bilges or the odd habits of the boom or the risk of deck slime upsetting the unwary. Other vessels might not always behave as they should or as expected.

Before the wide availability of tide tables seamen would have to know and understand this most important feature of their sailing lives. The basic pattern of twice daily ebb and flow in a twenty-eight-day cycle would be ingrained, and they would understand the influence of the moon, if not that of the sun, and would link low pressure characteristics to the tendency towards higher than usual tides. Slack water periods at the top and bottom of the tide, and such variations as spring and neap tides would all be very real factors. For the brief high of a spring tide in a month might just make the difference to having enough water to get over a bar or reach the staithe up a small coastal creek. The wrong wind could rob a vessel of steerage way, missing a tide could mean a tiresome wait, while every so often a combination of bad conditions could mean dropping every anchor available and just hoping things would improve before the grub ran out. The fire hazard and being caught by the wind too close to a lee shore were two of the most frequent dangers.

The individual vessel rigs determined their speed and handling characteristics. The traditional trow was originally limited by its single square sail which supplemented tidal movement and added an extra measure of manoeuvrability, but it was never much more than a tidal barge. The ketch rig's mizzen addition made it handier and faster. Their foresails would also add to the pulling power and a headsail with a 'horse' boom was a great boon for turning and extracting extra leverage from the wind. Topsails meant more speed but more work, and no crew was ever short of that. In light winds a topsail on a boom would be rigged above the mainsail and a flying jib used at the end of the bowsprit. Having the mizzen mast forward of the steering post helped in the balance of the boat and increased its manoeuvrability. When changing course or tacking, the jib fulfilled an important function in helping the vessel go through the eye of the wind, when disaster might otherwise result from being 'caught in stays' and losing headway off a dangerous coast or among shoals.

Sailing vessel rig was made up of standing rigging including shrouds to support the mast plus braces for the bowsprit, and of running rigging. The latter embraced the ropes and halyards used to hoist or lower sails to the required position, and other ropes that controlled the sails, the 'sheets'. Along with anchor chains, mooring lines – warps – and the like, much was required in the way of the skills for handling them.

Spare sail would need to be carried, even if it was only something bought second-hand off a larger vessel. Among the essential equipment were the working kedge and heavy bow anchors together with their chains, mooring and other ropes and warps, fenders, planks, boathooks, wheelbarrow, shovels and baskets and, of course, a few basic tools. Also essential were some spare timbers and some nails, some waterproof sheeting or tarpaulin, together with needle and thread and other small items such as a caulking hammer, grease, lamps, fuel for the pressure stove and the like.

Bacon, potatoes, onions, bread, milk, water and tea would be the essential provisions. The 'heads' needed a bucket added to the essentials list for an earthy purpose sometimes alluded to as 'bucket and chuck it'! The bilge pump might also need a bit of help from bucket work, especially when heavy seas were breaking.

Less obvious qualities required of our sailing forebears arose from the peculiarities associated with the varying different cargoes. Coal was a dirty product and when dropped into the hold from a chute or wagon tippler threw up a great cloud of dust that penetrated everywhere. The larger ports might have more sophisticated loading chutes to reduce the drop, the coal degradation and the dust, but they rarely offered a quick turnaround. Indeed, around 1880 it appears that the turnaround time for sailing ships loading in the docks at Cardiff could be as much as twelve days which pushed up the vessel's costs enormously. Even when loaded, the cargo still had to be trimmed to ensure the stability of the vessel and while the shipper would arrange for the harbour team to do this at the larger coal ports, other cargoes and other ports might well mean that the trimming had to be done by the vessel's crew. By the time this was done everyone would be not only tired but very dirty.

There would still be the unloading to come, which in many cases meant the work of shovelling into a basket and winching overboard or barrowing along some unsteady plank to the banks of a pill. Stone or sand might just be shovelled or thrown overside from the top of a load, but the lower the level became the harder the work. And when the area below the hatch had been cleared the remaining cargo might have to be moved to get it below the winch. A good team could unload 100 tons in a day, but where they had to be hired the cost might be as much as 2/6d a ton. At least one vessel, desperate for a load, is known to have got only 2/9d a ton for it. Bricks and other heavy materials had to be stowed carefully and evenly or the first load might just embed the vessel in the mud, an unwelcome event which might mean serious delay in sailing or even damage to the hull.

The duration of an individual voyage was not the sole working period. On shore there was the presentation or disposal of the cargo to be arranged, along with the relevant documentation. Making small repairs, restocking with supplies and the like involved the host of chandlers, agents, provision stores, customs, port officials and the harbour master. Tackling dirt, vermin, a dirty fuel pump or frayed halyard … the list was endless.

Although the custom and excise function did not greatly affect local trading vessels, there were many revenue cutters and bases in local waters, including this watch house near the Hung Road at Pill.

Until the later years of the sailing vessel trade, paperwork was not a major factor in the crew's lives. The revenue forces were generally concerned with bigger matters and the Letpass system sufficed for vessels on local runs, most of whom would be known to customs officers anyway and generally allowed to get on with their business without hindrance. Official oversight became more of a factor as a result of the Merchant Shipping Acts of 1894 and 1906 and their provisions relating to coastal trading vessels of over 15 tons burden. These required that such vessels had to be registered and the certificate of registry produced on demand, along with bills of lading and cargo manifests. It became an offence to overload a vessel dangerously or stow the load badly so as to be a danger, with masters and owners liable to prosecution if that occurred. Lifesaving equipment also had to be provided, although the local channel vessels had always carried a small boat for towing, mooring and other running about.

The whole picture was that of an incredibly skilful life of extremely hard work and great risks, all done for modest reward, but all making the past sailors of local waters unacknowledged masters, and often heroes, of their trade. It was a dangerous business, and many paid the price of their life for their dedication to the sea, but some continued the sailing that was their art right into their 80s, sometimes in vessels half as old again.

5. INLAND WATERS

As shipping business into Somerset's coastal harbours grew, so did the proportion moving inland for the hinterland towns and villages, as did the inland produce flowing out to more distant markets. Until the growth of the railway system in the second half of the nineteenth century quite a substantial proportion of this onward movement passed by water, initially along natural rivers and then along canalised routes. From inland centres, especially Langport, distribution of coal, salt, building materials and the more general merchandise, could then be made by packhorse or wagon organised by a host of agents, merchants and chapmen. In terms of importance and activity, the River Parrett network and its River Tone connecting route to Taunton were the most significant, with lesser but quite wide-ranging movements along the River Axe. The River Brue did provide a way from Bridgwater Bay to Glastonbury, but it had significant shortcomings which the Glastonbury Canal attempted, with limited and short-lived success, to overcome.

Behind this general overview lie several qualifications. In early centuries the main one was the problem of keeping navigations clear of vegetation and with adequate depths. The obligation to do this lay with the landowner, but he had to be constantly balancing his need for water for livestock, his desire to keep the land moist but drained and use it productively, and the actual cost of clearing weeds and silt. Even the authoritarian abbots of Glastonbury had to balance the value of waterways for moving produce with the water demands of the mills for which they were also landlords. The mills themselves were in frequent conflict over their water needs and were not well-liked by fishermen either. In later years the drainage commissioners and the landowners who provided their funds also had rather different priorities.

Small vessels and varied cargoes penetrated for a limited distance up the minor rivers of North Somerset, notably the Yeo and Banwell. Inland water transport really came into its own in the low-lying area south of the Mendip range. There, the River Axe followed its meandering course via Lympsham, Bleadon and Lower Weare, then south of Axbridge and Cheddar and on to Clewer and Bleadney

Bridge. As part of drainage improvements along the original course of the Axe, cut-offs isolated two loops on the first section, affecting the age-old Hobbs Boat ferry and the one at White House Farm on the road south from Loxton to Rooks Bridge. The Axe's Yeo tributary ran closer to the Mendip heights of Wavering Down via Rackley and Cross and on to Hythe which may once have been part of a water route for access to Cheddar.

The coal wharf at Lympsham was the last to remain in use on the Axe after, first, the 1802 drainage legislation which resulted in a sluice at Bleadon and no access upriver from there, and then the 1841 arrival of the Bristol & Exeter Railway which crossed the Axe between these two villages. Previously, quite small boats had been active on the higher reaches since medieval times with simple wharves

The original course of the River Axe and once the site of the White House Ferry. (Roy Gallop)

to serve the small townships, hamlets and farmsteads. Lower down, 11-ton coal barges brought their cargoes up to places like Cross and Weare.

The waterway pattern in this whole area used to be quite different to that of today. The River Brue once flowed north to join the Axe at Bleadney before being diverted more directly towards the sea during the thirteenth century. This was the period of the making of the Pilrow Cut which gave another route to and from Glastonbury via Mark to join the former great loop of the Axe south of Loxton. The waterway rights of the abbot of Glastonbury were the major influence in these changes, the great abbey having tremendous expertise in drainage, land reclamation and in using natural waterways for moving people and produce and keeping the abbey and its satellites supplied. Its inspections and communications were often by boat and its officials had specific duties such as the transport of the abbey's wine supply.

In the period between the end of the Glastonbury Abbey influence and the cut-offs and other water control measures of the nineteenth century, the national population increased rapidly, raising the demand for food to feed it. Farming changed to reflect this with more land under cultivation, better ways of using it and a rising demand not only for the transport of produce but also in the appetite for goods that would formerly have been rare luxuries. Wines, spices, oats and pottery joined the staples of salt, livestock and fuel in reaching places that horse transport could not effectively or economically serve. Significantly, two early small canals were cut for the purpose of supplying manure for the land.

The Brue remained a secondary route, primarily because it flowed from and through sparsely-inhabited moorland, whereas the Axe served countless modest-sized communities, including Axbridge and Cheddar. As coal supplanted peat for non-domestic use, the activity along the Axe further increased. Wharf remains confirm small waterway loading and unloading points at places like Clewer, once the top of the tide, and Hythe. On the Yeo tributary at Rackley there was a papal reference to the 'portu de Radeclive' as early as 1179 and an attempt to create a township there, possibly to improve access for the upriver trade to Axbridge and Cheddar. Later, coal for Compton Bishop and for local farms arrived at the simple wharf at Rackley, which also handled incoming slates for some of the local houses. Odd cargoes of Shipham calamine may also have gone downriver, even cloth and corn for distant destinations.

The medieval town of Weare was founded in the late twelfth century and, as elsewhere along the Axe, the port connection is confirmed by several local field names. There was a significant early water route along the Axe and then south through Rooksbridge and Mark to Meare Pool via the Pilrow Cut. Pottery which originated at Nether Stowey has been found at Rooksbridge, but no trace of the probable wharf there. Bleadney seems insignificant now, but would have

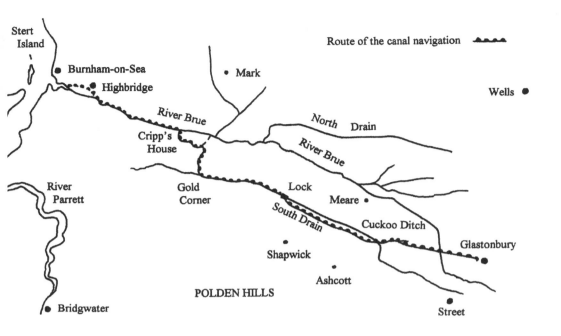

The Glastonbury Canal, which made use of the lower section of the River Brue and then the South Drain, was eventually sold to the Somerset Central Railway which used much of its course for the railway trackbed.

had a much better water flow when it had the water supply of both the Brue and the Axe.

The River Brue was used quite intensively for the short distance up to the railway wharf at Highbridge, but the Glastonbury Canal proved a doomed venture provoking the eventual suicide of one of its backers and the defaulting flight of another. It was based on a contrived route from a sea lock at Highbridge via the River Brue, the Cripps River and the South Drain to an awkward approach to Glastonbury along Cuckoo Brook and Mill Stream. The works at Highbridge were difficult and costly. Some sections of the waterway were not puddled properly and water leakage gradually restricted its use.

Although useful to their immediate communities, the River Brue and the River Axe and the latter's connections were of relatively minor significance compared with the importance of the River Parrett, its River Tone link to Taunton and its several other lesser tributaries. These penetrated into the very heart of Somerset and provided an effective way of supplying its communities with the whole range of goods coming into Bridgwater and transhipped there into barges to complete their journey. These rivers also allowed the inland communities to export their produce on a scale that would not have been possible using packhorses or wagons.

The tides dictated movement on the lower Parrett as far as its junction with the Tone. Below Bridgwater the narrow pill at Combwich gave access to traffic for and from Cannington, Stogursey and the surrounding area while the wharf at Dunball not only provided a connection with the Bristol & Exeter Railway after its opening in 1841, but could also be used when depths, icing and other limitations prevented normal access to Bridgwater. On the other side of

The substantial building of Thorney Mill on the upper reaches of the River Parrett. Adjoining the mill are the remains of the old lock and the sluices which were vital to maintaining an adequate depth of water upriver.

Bridgwater, upriver from the Parrett–Tone junction at Stanmoor, the barges had to forsake tidal movement for the use of towing horses stabled there, with this pattern being reversed in the downstream direction.

The Parrett was bridged at Langport as early as the thirteenth century. The Great Bow Bridge replacement followed in the fifteenth, but its low arches precluded the 20-ton barges from Bridgwater continuing upriver. Coal, salt and much of the shipment tonnage arriving at Langport was unloaded for local use or to go into storage pending later sale and onward movement by packhorse or wagon. From the quay and warehouses on the north bank of the river and just downstream of the bridge, some of this tonnage was then sent forward to a surprisingly large number of townships in the surrounding areas of Somerset and even beyond the county boundaries.

Goods moving beyond Langport by water involved the awkward process of transhipment to smaller barges of 5–10 tons for conveyance to places like Thorney Mill further along the Parrett and, occasionally, a short way along the River Isle. Movement along the Yeo/Ivel to Ilchester can be traced back to Roman times, but depths beyond Load Bridge, which regularly unloaded coal and culm, were often inadequate. On this last stretch barges sometimes managed to get as far as a small basin by the old packhorse Pill Bridge, a little way outside Ilchester.

Improving this access to Ilchester was the objective of the Company of Proprietors of the Navigation from Ivelchester to Langport which obt0ained its Act of Parliament in June 1795. Sadly its dream ended six years later with the coffers empty and only a small amount of construction at the Langport end completed. Better fortune attended the Westport Canal, a 2½-mile link from the River Isle to a basin and warehouses at Westport from which goods could be moved on by road to places like Barrington, Ilminster and South Petherton.

The Westport Canal and waterway improvements beyond Langport were a supplementary feature of the wider scheme authorised by the Parrett Navigation Act of 1836. This was designed to improve the river downstream from Langport and to aid and stimulate the substantial trade already carried. It provided for locks at each end of the Stanmoor to Langport section plus a further lock at Oath, designed to produce improvements in and greater control over the highly variable water supply and consequent river depths. Another major feature of the legislation was the replacement of the former restrictive bridge at Langport. The river improvements part had been completed by 1838 and the new bridge some fifteen months later. Traffic at this period amounted to some 55,000 tons per annum and the expectation was that the lock tolls plus a special temporary charge for crossing the bridge would recoup the £42,000 construction costs involved. Over the next few years the amount of traffic increased by some 20 per cent, but this prosperity began to decline after the opening of the branch railway from Taunton to Yeovil in 1853.

The River Parrett and former sluices at Langport with the old Parrett Navigation lock and toll collector's house beyond the small island.

The River Tone wanders its way through Taunton Deane and the county town itself before joining the Parrett at Stanmoor. As early as 1638 it had been made navigable between that point and Ham Mills just outside Taunton and before the end of that century was bringing significant quantities of seaborne coal from the channel to be carried by packhorses for the last 3 miles into Taunton proper. By 1717 the whole length had been provided with further locks to enable small barges to bring in Swansea coal transhipped at Bridgwater. Other goods also contributed to the steady rise in annual tonnages and the revenues of the Conservators of the Tone, with some quite significant dividends being paid out. The undertaking was important, useful and quite substantial in that it had four conventional locks and a similar number of half-locks.

A major change in the water route to Taunton arose from a complexity of grandiose schemes put forward for a ship canal. This was a part of an age-old dream of linking the Bristol and English channels to avoid the long sea journey around Cornwall and had several permutations including one to link Bristol with Exeter. The debates over each scheme raged quite fiercely at times. Emerging from these various promotions came the Bridgwater & Taunton Canal, which would, and did from 1827, provide an easier and more direct route to Taunton than that via the two rivers. After some in-fighting the canal company and the Tone Conservators came to an accommodation and coal continued to move via the Tone for some time.

Prompted by the advantages brought by the new Bridgwater–Taunton waterway, a scheme for a link to Ilminster and Chard followed and produced an Act for a canal of some 13½ miles from a junction with its ally at Creech St Michael in 1834. It was a difficult undertaking necessitating tunnels and inclined planes and using small tub boats, 26ft long and designed to be hauled up and down the inclines by means of a caisson or trolley running on rails. The troubled undertaking finally reached Chard in 1842 to enjoy some initial success, again by the dramatic impact of cheaper coal prices.

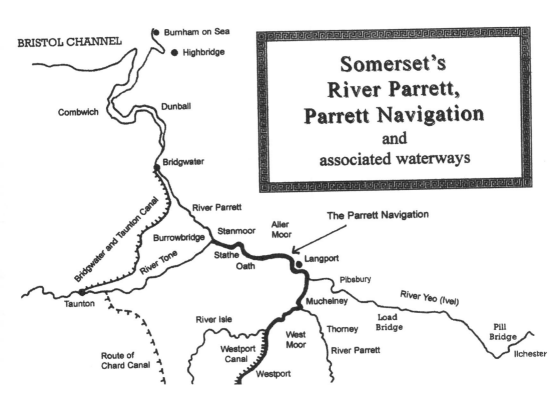

In 1841 the Bridgwater & Taunton Canal was extended from its former Bridgwater basin at Huntworth, around the town of Bridgwater, to a new dock on the Parrett and downstream of the town bridge. Significantly, this was also the year in which the probing Bristol & Exeter Railway had arrived on its southward path to Exeter and spelled the eventual end of the good years on these water routes to and via Taunton. The Parrett Navigation suffered the same fate after the railway branch to Yeovil opened, while the Glastonbury Canal had to endure the indignity of purchase, closure and conversion to provide trackbed land for its railway usurper. After twenty-five years from its opening in 1842, the Chard Canal went the same way and was sold to its railway rival for £5,945, a fraction of its construction cost.

THE LANGPORT BOATMAN

We're completely free, the barge and me,
In tune with the tide and the weather,
From Langport Quay to the salt of the sea,
In harmony together.

We work up the Yeo, to Westport we go,
Anywhere on the Parrett, Tone or Isle,
Any creek, pill or rhyne will do us just fine,
And we'll get there by skill, luck or guile.

From a boy of just eight, I've worked dawn 'till late,
To learn every trick of the stream,
Stuckey's Bank made a loan, now the barge is my own,
And at last I am living my dream.

I've a mate, of course, and a boy with a horse,
But my biggest friend is the tide,
High, low, slack or neap, we need three foot deep,
And our sweeps, sail, and a chain overside.

Welsh coal means you sweat, hay mustn't get wet,
There are withies and stone for the taking,
But as Bow Bridge appears, and the journey's end nears,
You forget that your muscles are aching.

I admit there are days when the job hardly pays,
And the cargoes are scarce, wet or heavy,
But the barge is now mine and we do just fine,
Even after the 'Nav' takes its levy.

Though the railway gets near, I'll stay of good cheer,
And barge on through sun, wind and rain,
If things go awry, I can always apply,
For a new job – of driving a train!

Geoff Body

PART 2

Ports, Pills and Wharves

6. NORTH SOMERSET

Apart from the considerable shipping activity and settlements around the mouth of the River Avon, the remainder of the coast as far as the entrance to the River Axe, together with its immediate hinterland, was essentially a pastoral, self-sufficient area until the coming of the railways. No doubt the odd early cargo was landed on beaches or in pill entrances, some passed up the Yeo and Banwell rivers and other modest waterways and some coal continued to be brought in to places like Clevedon and Congresbury, especially for small manufacturers and bulk users like gas works. Some produce was forwarded by sea to Bristol and occasional loads became available for special works such as the movement of stone for sea defences.

Crockerne Pill, now known simply as Pill, had centuries of providing channel pilots and their cutters and the hobblers who toiled at their oars to tow vessels up the Avon. Opposite the earlier docks at Avonmouth, the southern mouth of the river where it reaches the estuary is now the site of the modern Royal Portbury Dock. Further on, the creek wharf at Portishead was used by local fishermen and others and has survived the era of the town's docks development and the considerable power station coal, Albright & Wilson chemicals and the timber wharf traffic handled there. Now all the traditional dock activity has been replaced by the large marina and housing development which has taken place around the dock waters.

Thanks to its sheltered position in the lee of Brean Down the pill off the River Axe at Uphill has a long history of sailing vessel movements, once Welsh cattle for fattening and later coal, salt and general cargoes inwards and stone, bricks and lime outwards. And the activity did not end there for small craft went surprisingly long distances up the Axe until drainage sluices put an end to this age-old practice.

Further back in time, before the pattern of waterways was changed by drainage schemes, a waterway route to Glastonbury existed via the Axe and the connecting link to the Brue via the Pilrow Cut.

Well before the resort of Weston-super-Mare emerged from its humble origins in the nineteenth century, Uphill was the most important shipping location between the River Avon and the mouth of the River Parrett.

Pill

Originally and more properly known as Crockerne Pill, this large village is situated on the south bank of the River Avon, not far from its mouth. Although only a few miles from Bristol, it was largely self-contained and self-sufficient until the second half of the eighteenth century, for only a difficult and circuitous horse track connected the village with its busy and important neighbour. The modest inlet at Pill was fed by a small stream and provided a shelter for pilot cutters and other small boats, while the larger sea-going merchantmen could moor up to the low cliffs just upstream to wait for tide and towing or to tranship their cargoes to and from lighters. Naval vessels also used these moorings, known as the Hung Road as mooring hawsers could be attached to the cliff face.

Early pilot cutters were built at Bristol, but for many years subsequently local boatbuilders, Rowles, Cooper and others, built fast and extremely seaworthy pilot cutters at Pill, and the community there reared the men who sailed them. They

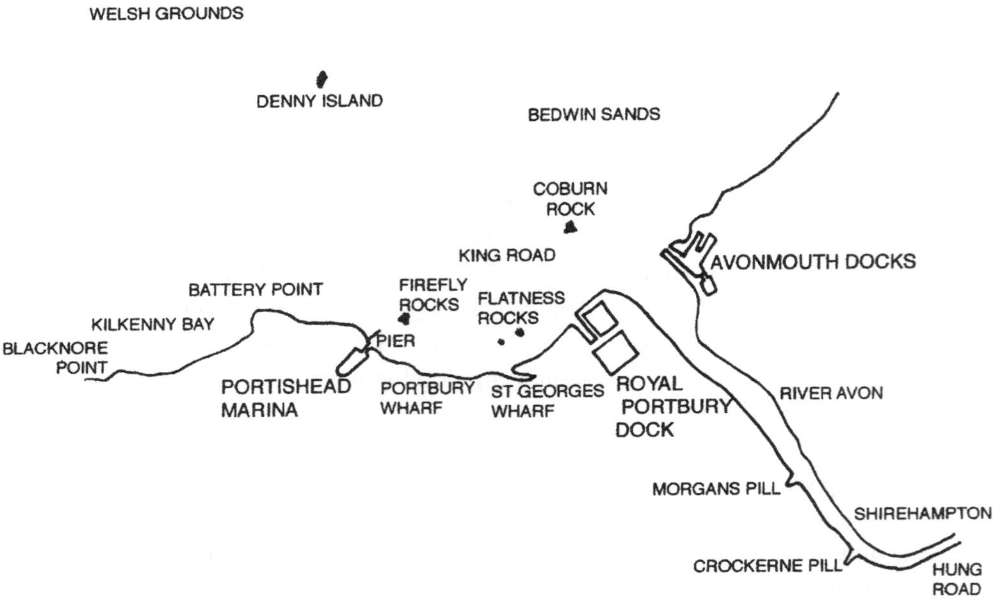

WELSH GROUNDS

DENNY ISLAND

BEDWIN SANDS

COBURN ROCK

KING ROAD

AVONMOUTH DOCKS

BATTERY POINT

FIREFLY ROCKS

FLATNESS ROCKS

KILKENNY BAY

BLACKNORE POINT

PIER

PORTISHEAD MARINA

PORTBURY WHARF

ST GEORGES WHARF

ROYAL PORTBURY DOCK

RIVER AVON

MORGANS PILL

SHIREHAMPTON

CROCKERNE PILL

HUNG ROAD

went out in all weathers to await the merchantmen arriving with supplies for Bristol's growing port and population and for those heading to Gloucester or the South Wales harbours. From 1861 Cardiff, Newport and Gloucester began to share in this pilotage activity and fierce competition could often occur.

In the heyday of sail an incoming ship had to take on a pilot once past Lundy and the cutters would race out there, and often further, to earn their ten guineas pilotage fee. From 1891 the compulsory pilotage boundary was altered to Flatholm. Before getting their certificate, aspiring pilots had to spend at least seven years learning the waters as westermen, or Western Men. Their job was to bring the cutter back, with just a boy to help, once the pilot had transferred to his seagoing charge.

Pill village also provided the hobblers and towing teams to haul vessels up the tidal Avon and moor them at the Bristol quays until the advent of steam tugs gradually made the boats, rowers and horses redundant. At one time oxen were used for the towing task, one naval vessel in 1630 needing 'eight tow-boats and sixty yoke of oxen' to clear the River Avon.

In medieval times there was some shipping trade in pottery from nearby Ham Green, but there was hardly any industry at Pill and the locally-produced supplies it provided for passing deep sea ships were transferred by small boat. Some goods came ashore this way from vessels waiting in the Hung Road, but a watchful customs post tried valiantly to ensure duty was paid. There was a customs presence at Pill from 1693 and the watch house, which comprised working and living quarters for the local revenue men, still exists there.

Not that all was sweetness and light. Both pilots and hobblers were a competitive bunch and depended on being tough and active to reach and persuade shipmasters to take on their services. When vessels in the Hung Road obstructed the task of the hobblers strong words would be exchanged. Pill itself catered for the needs of its own and visiting seafarers for drink, tobacco and other pleasures denied them at sea. But none of the various small excesses and disturbances compared with the activities of one local man named Morgan whose infamy may well be perpetuated in the name of a small creek just downstream from the main village.

Morgan and his son were a thorn in the flesh of the Bristol authorities throughout the first half of the seventeenth century. The father seems to have been at odds with the Corporation of Bristol for twenty years or more, with his son then taking the same course to such effect that a petition against his behaviour was sent to the Privy Council in 1630. He was accused of removing mooring posts to build a personal stronghold by the river at Pill and there running eleven pothouses which offered tobacco and strong beer to all and sundry, to the detriment of both morals and behaviour.

The Archbishop of York and the Chief Justice of the Court of Common Pleas were deputed to investigate, a commission which involved them in heading down the Avon in boats laden with 'roast beef, pies, sweetmeats, cakes and wine'. Thus fortified, they duly condemned Morgan's actions, but any change seems to have been slow and small for it took another petition in 1637 to secure any measure of compliance. Even then the younger Morgan went down fighting with a complaint about his treatment to the House of Commons in 1641. Clearly Pill was a place of maritime importance and had its own idea of independence.

Today, the once-busy ferry across to the slipway by the Lamplighters Inn on the other side of the Avon at Shirehampton no longer carries crowds of local workers, and modest and muddy Morgan's Pill just downstream is the only reminder of this colourful character. The tiny inlet there once featured as the northern end of a scheme for a canal south to Bridgwater and Taunton. Forgotten too is the National Shipyard Company's prospective shipyard just beyond Morgan's Pill. This project originated in 1917 out of the need to replace wartime shipping losses. To cater for the materials of construction a new signal box, three loop lines and a branch towards the river were built a little way along the main railway

Low tide at Pill, looking across the River Avon to Shirehampton. In earlier times this little harbour would have been crowded with pilot cutters and the hobblers' rowing boats.

line towards Portishead, and a modest new station opened in 1918 to serve the
workers. The yard was abandoned incomplete in 1921 and its station closed two
years later.

Royal Portbury Dock

This impressive development, built over a five-year period from 1972 on a virgin
site on the southern side of the mouth of the Avon, is rather outside the scope
and purpose of this book, but needs brief mention because of its importance and
for the sake of being comprehensive. Operated by the Bristol Port Company,
it is now a major port and has the largest entrance lock in the UK. The lock's
951ft length and 135ft width permit the accommodation of the very large bulk
carrier vessels which bring in substantial numbers of cars and high volumes of
coal and aviation fuel. Containers and timber are also major imports and there are
forwardings of wheat and motor vehicles.

Portishead

The nineteenth century brought great change to Portishead. Its location on
the widening estuary beyond the mouth of the River Avon had given the small
agricultural settlement links with the sea for hundreds of years, but the tidal creek
which probed inland as far as the former mill that became the White Lion Inn
was used only by the numerous local fishing vessels and small trading craft. By the
end of the eighteenth century several market boats regularly took fish, corn, cider
and other produce up the Avon to Bristol, and various types of building materials
were brought in for local development on the return voyage. The proximity
of Portishead to the King Road where larger vessels sheltered, waited for the
tide or transhipped cargoes probably meant that the local people sometimes got
involved in less respectable activities. An early watch house was located there and
preventive officers were active.

Once the nation's economy had recovered from the crippling cost of the
Napoleonic Wars, activity around Portishead increased. It was selected by the City
of Bristol for development as a seaside resort which would be a major amenity
for its citizens. Money was invested in landholdings and plans were prepared in
1828 for a hotel which was duly opened in 1831 with a landing stage nearby. A
regular packet boat service operated to and from Bristol so that visitors could
enjoy the Royal Hotel and its gardens, landing its passengers at the parish wharf at
high tide and near the hotel when the water was lower and continuing to operate
until the coming of the railway. The area suffered a setback when attempts to
secure government investment failed and nothing came of Brunel's plans to
make Portishead a terminal for his *Great Western* steamship. These were, however,
years of stuttering growth, albeit just through more visitors by steamer initially.
There were several schemes for piers and one for an atmospheric railway link

with Bristol which was to be provided with an incline up to the embryo Clifton Suspension Bridge.

The second half of the nineteenth century brought tangible improvements in the access to Portishead. The Bristol & Portishead Pier and Railway Company opened its line from Bristol in April 1867 and added a new rail-connected pier for good measure. Vessels like the *Eagle*, *Cambria* and *Saint David* were now calling regularly at the pier and for many years provided Bristolians with an excursion to enjoy the sea air, and another steamer operated to and from Cardiff. Another notable event was the arrival of a former naval eighty-four-gun two-decker in September 1869. The 64-year-old warship was moored to the north-west of the pier and was used to provide worthwhile training for poor, wayward or abandoned boys off the streets of Bristol. Soon filled with nearly a hundred lads, TS *Formidable* fulfilled this role, with the help of the brigantine *Polly* which was purchased for use as a tender and to provide lessons in practical seamanship, until the activity moved to a fine new nautical school ashore in 1906.

Despite a host of different voices representing the Bristol involvement and rivalries with the plans for the new docks at Avonmouth, Portishead secured massive investment from the Bristol docks estate surplus in 1873. Then, finally, and ten years after the arrival of the *Formidable*, Portishead got a fine new dock built over the former marsh and very much in the form it has remained, albeit now serving a different function.

Inevitably, its location on the approaches to the River Avon and the docks of Bristol meant that Portishead's development was always going to be linked with that city and its maritime activity. A nineteenth-century example of this was the building nearby of a quarantine hospital specifically for housing contagious cases among passengers on vessels destined for Bristol. They were brought ashore at Portishead under special arrangements to allow the vessel to be cleared for the final leg of its journey. Isolation, treatment and working in the gardens were then the programme. Later the hospital became a farm school for youngsters destined for emigration.

The main-line railway, now part of the Great Western Railway, steadily increased its siding access to the dock and was joined by the Weston, Clevedon & Portishead Railway which reached Portishead in 1907 and was linked to the Great Western Railway and the docks in the following years. The rail traffic reflected the principal activities of the port with some coal arriving and some timber being moved forward for inland destinations.

The twentieth century also brought further expansion in the form of a BP oil installation and then an electricity power station which came on stream in 1929 and was fed by a succession of steam and motor colliers. The dock had a busy Second World War, storing military supplies and getting bombed for its trouble. Subsequently a second power station, Portishead B, was commissioned in 1955,

The pier and lock entrance at Portishead. The small, slate-roofed brick building on the left was formerly the lock keeper's office..

both stations on the north side of the dock. There, too, were the attendant coal discharge quays, storage areas and wagon tipplers although the B station was also oil burning. Beyond the power stations the railway sidings continued towards Bailey's maize mill and the substantial lock gates and entrance chamber and to the pier railway station. The latter closed in 1954 in favour of a new station nearer the town, but this was only to last for ten years.

The south side berths of the dock handled timber at No. 1 Wharf, wood pulp and oil at No. 2 with No. 3 the location of the hydraulic arms that directed liquid phosphorus to the conveyors into Albright & Wilson's factory, built early in the 1950s and lasting until 1969.

The last decades of the century brought the end of the former dock and industrial complex. Railway services were withdrawn, the two power stations were closed and demolished and the docks closed to shipping altogether in 1992. Stagnation in the dock area followed, but the millennium heralded a new chapter

Replaced by a marina and new housing, the old dock at Portishead is seen from the original parish wharf.

with the construction of a new lock barrel being followed by the opening in 2001 of the Portishead Quays marina. In the new century Portishead's links with the sea were thus secure in the marina and its wealth of surrounding developments and in the survival of the old parish wharf which has been protected and transformed by community-prompted action.

The dock entrance at Portishead looks out to the approaches to Avonmouth Docks and the modern Royal Portbury Dock. Between Portishead and the latter is a lonely, muddy shoreline where narrow tracks still lead to the old St George's and Portbury wharves. This whole waterside area, from Pill to Easton-in-Gordano, was home to numerous Second World War defence sites, especially anti-aircraft batteries, all designed to defend Avonmouth Docks and the seaward approaches to Bristol. Also now absorbed into the landscape around the former Portishead Docks are the pond reservoirs for surplus water from the old power stations which once more play a useful role as part of a wildlife habitat.

Clevedon

Until the nineteenth century, Clevedon and its surrounding area consisted of little more than a small fishing community and a collection of scattered farms. There were only eighty houses in the village in 1630 and that number did not rise above a hundred until the early 1800s. Growth was then quite rapid from about 1820 onwards with better roads, a coach service to Bristol and then a railway branch from the main line of the Bristol & Exeter Railway. The former self-sufficiency based on home-grown produce, kiln lime from local quarries and some small boat fishing was replaced by more exotic supplies brought in from Bristol to cater for the substantial dwellings erected. Hotels, inns and then a pier catered for the increasing number of visitors.

Clevedon Bay was not a welcoming place for coastal shipping so such activity as there was took place at the pill at the older, southern end of the town. There, sheltered by Church Hill, a group of minor rivers and a major drainage channel reach the sea creeks, but even here high water depths can often be less than a metre. The Land Yeo, the Middle Yeo and the Blind Yeo were hardly significant water highways, although the odd small smack may have made odd visits to the little inlet and moved a short distance inland and there would have been some transhipment to small local boats able to penetrate further.

By the late nineteenth century coal merchant George Thomas was advertising 'Best Coals from the Forest of Dean' which arrived in his own vessels and could be delivered at 25/- a ton. Mrs Thomas is recorded as the owner of the coal sloop *Liver*. The coal could be unloaded at a simple wharf beside the pill and weighed over the local weighbridge. The 'hard' built under the shadow of the hill allowed access for the horse and cart drivers to collect their loads for delivery in the main town. In the opposite direction, stone quarried at the nearby Wains Hill Quarry was loaded into trows and, like that from Uphill, used in the construction of the sea wall at Kingston Seymour.

The last seaborne coal arrived in Clevedon during the Second World War, but earlier the Rowles brothers variously owned and operated several vessels at Clevedon in the decades before and after 1900. These included the trows *Brothers*, *William and Martha* and *Nellie* and the ketch *Emily*. Another small cargo activity was salt produced by evaporation on the Salthouse Field and said to have provided an occasional load for a vessel called the *Little Harp* which foundered in Salthouse Bay not far from the hostelry now bearing its name, but this is the subject of conflicting stories.

Pleasure and excursion sailings using a rescued and restored Clevedon Pier continue to be substantial and important but, apart from that wartime load of coal, the last traditional maritime activity around the pill was ship-breaking which ended in the 1930s. John Hurley broke up Pockett's notable paddle steamer *Velindra* at the hard after she was scrapped in 1897 and the 172-ton iron paddler

Small pleasure craft lie quietly in the entrance to the Yeo rivers at Clevedon. Quite large vessels used to be broken up here.

Ira in 1908. Captain Rowles was also extensively involved in ship-breaking, albeit later, and the pill was the graveyard for a host of barges, ketches and schooners over a period of some forty years.

Woodspring Bay and Sand Bay

The coastal areas of the Kingston Seymour and Wick St Lawrence parishes are still relatively remote. They are low-lying, honeycombed with waterways and, before modern drainage, were liable to great and frequent flooding. Farms, rhynes and pasture predominate with the Kenn, Yeo and Banwell rivers collecting the waters of lesser streams on their way to Woodspring Bay. Channel vessels sailed by in great numbers and over the centuries many a small craft would occasionally have landed goods at suitable spots along this lonely shore. Not all would have been on legitimate business, for the area had a reputation for smuggling. Indeed, apart from farming, the only other occupation of note among past villagers in Wick St Lawrence was that of coastguard, and an obsolete cutter moored at the entrance to the Yeo was the base for preventative officers at one period.

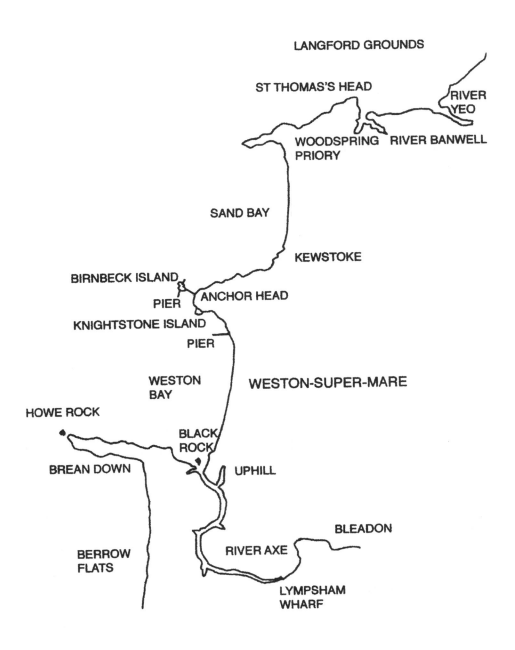

On the empty grasslands between Weston-super-Mare and Clevedon the remains of the Weston, Clevedon & Portishead Railway's coal unloading jetty on the River Yeo are still visible.

It is easy to imagine a time when the odd load of contraband would be landed in this remote entrance to the Banwell River.

The tiny Kingston Pill is too far from anywhere to have warranted trading activity, but the sea wall to the south was built with stone brought from the quarry at Uphill by trow and there were certainly some movements along the River Yeo. An article in the *South Avon Mercury* mentions barges being loaded with ore from Wrington at a wharf near the Ship and Castle at Congresbury.

The River Yeo was certainly used to land coal brought in for the Weston, Clevedon & Portishead Railway, one of several light railways of character which came to be managed by the redoubtable Col H.F. Stephens. A simple jetty and wharf was built where the railway crossed the river and was provided with a short spur off the running line to handle the occasional coal shipments arriving from around 1914. The colonel then came to believe that savings could be made for his impecunious line by bringing its coal supplies across the Bristol Channel in its own vessel. Accordingly the *Sarah*, a smack-rigged trow built in 1873 at Framilode, was purchased and brought her first load of coal for unloading at the Yeo wharf in 1924. Three years later the 1897 Penrhyn-built 60-ton *Lily* took over the monthly load, but sank during a nightmare voyage in 1929. The ketch *Edith* was also employed occasionally. A steam crane was used for discharging these vessels for a time, but later this had to be done by using the vessel's derrick.

Another use of the River Yeo is recorded back in the 1720s and '30s when William Donne had a vessel bringing iron in bar or plate form from Bristol to his mill at Congresbury. In a process called 'splitting', this raw material was converted to rods for use in nail-making. Some use might also have been made of the river's minor tributary, the Oldbridge River, which gave access for very small craft to Puxton.

At the southern end of Woodspring Bay the River Banwell emerges at a spot sheltered by St Thomas's Head, itself the site of an MoD establishment which undertook experimental work until fairly recently. Woodspring Priory could have been supplied via a short pill off the Banwell and goods could also have been transhipped to small craft for the St George's and Banwell communities. Along the Middle Hope stretch of coast to Sand Point, Hope Cove had a smuggling reputation, complete with a supposed tunnel to spirit the spirits away.

Around Sand Point lies the long sweep of Sand Bay with Kewstoke village stretched out below Worlebury Hill. The name Kewstoke may have its roots in the Celtic word for 'boat' and there used to be fishing for shrimps and sprats from near the present Commodore Hotel, itself formerly the site of two fishermen's cottages. The New Inn reputedly was involved in the odd bit of smuggling, especially casks of wine and spirits lobbed overboard from vessels on the Bordeaux–Bristol run and recovered from the beach after being stranded there by the tide that had floated them in. The shapes of ghostly horses and furtive men form part of local legend.

Weston-super-Mare

Before the nineteenth century there was little at Weston-super-Mare to suggest its eventual growth as a popular resort; such use as was made of the wide, shallow Weston Bay was by small fishing vessels with a single mast and small square sail. This was all they needed, for their activity rarely took them out of the bay into the more difficult waters beyond. Indeed, much of Weston's catch was taken quite close to the shore with 'callers' to scare away the gulls.

The development of Weston as a seaside town was then quite rapid from the 1820s and included the establishment of a bathhouse and pool on Knightstone Island which was opened in 1822. This provided an opportunity to create a small sheltered area in which vessels could unload their cargoes of coal, building materials and other goods as demand increased in line with the growth of the town.

A former Scottish ferry and a Dunkirk veteran in the shelter of Knightstone Harbour at Weston-super-Mare waiting for their busy season.

By the 1840s the visitors coming to Weston had created a demand for entertainment. Fishermen were glad to supplement their income by providing short summer trips, and tugs from Bristol quickly joined the trend. Temporarily modified for their new role, these embarked and landed their passengers at Birnbeck, Anchor Head or in the mouth of the River Axe at the south end of the bay. From this modest beginning sprang over a century of passenger steamer operation.

The Bristol & Exeter Railway's 1841 branch line into Weston-super-Mare was an unimpressive affair, just a single line from the direct route between Yatton and Bridgwater and operated for its first few years using spartan carriages drawn by horses. But the original 1841 station is illustrated with trucks and the primitive sheer legs cranes to unload them and would soon have been handling merchandise as well as passengers. Increasingly, the infant railway would have been used to bring in supplies of general merchandise from Bristol and the sea-going vessels discharging there. Some of the coal previously brought over to Weston and nearby Uphill by water would also be lost to rail, depending on how far it had to be carted and especially after the opening of the Severn Tunnel.

At low tide such cargoes as continued to come by sea could be unloaded on the harbour mud directly to the horse-drawn carts that would deliver them. Coal shipments were always a seasonal business, but Weston's modest harbour did have its busy periods, one illustration showing no less than five vessels of various rigs moored there, among them the Gloucester ketch *Eliza*. Although gradually giving way to land competition, some movements continued until the 1930s, but the activity was minor compared with the summer pleasure boating in fishing boats, launches and steamers.

Not that Weston was content with its marine facilities. No resort worthy of its name failed to want a pier and the long gestation of the scheme for one based on Birnbeck Island was begun in 1845, but not realised for over twenty years. In between there had been an 1854 plan for a railway-served jetty at Uphill followed in 1859 by a scheme to enclose a water area at the northern end of Weston Bay and provide it with a railway link from Puxton. Even more dramatic was an 1861 idea involving the creation of a full-scale harbour at the end of Brean Down, not a new concept, but one that now had national support and was seen as catering for international traffic as well as shorter distance mail and merchandise. It too would be served by a branch railway and work was actually begun, but was largely wrecked by a severe storm in 1872. Despite a reincarnation of the Brean Down Harbour project in 1887, a fresh Act of Parliament in 1889 and another extending the time limits in 1893, the wave-battered works were soon to be abandoned and the grand vision forgotten.

Although relatively few cargo vessels worked into and out of Weston, a great number passed by in the narrowing Bristol Channel and a lifeboat station established at Birnbeck in 1882 saved over a hundred lives in its first seventy-five years of service. The list of rescues features trows, ketches, schooners and a few steamships, reflecting the pattern of sailings to and from the larger channel ports.

Uphill and Lympsham

A deceptively small and meandering pill off the River Axe leads for 500 yards to a sluice protecting Weston's small village-cum-suburb of Uphill. Now a haven for small pleasure craft, the meeting point of pill and village was once the site of a busy wharf, quarry and limekiln area at Uphill which has a long history as a small coastal port. In addition to the local fishing activity off the Axe Estuary, small vessels could make their way up the main river and penetrate some distance inland by tortuous minor waterways, especially in the flooding periods.

Originally a manorial port, Uphill represented a harbour sheltered by the bulk of Brean Down and was the limit of the Port of Bristol's jurisdiction. For many years the pill had no public wharf and ancient rights made it one of the very small

With four 'properly' dressed passengers, the ferry from Brean nears the beach at Uphill after crossing the mouth of the River Axe.

number of free ports. Customs officers were based at Uphill from 1685 onwards, but some illicit activity had always taken place there and probably continued, albeit less openly.

Back in 1591 a French vessel, the *Gray Honde* of Bayonne, was brought into Uphill, having been 'furiouslye battered' and captured while on a return voyage from Newfoundland. Our quarrel at the time was with Spain and Portugal, but 'the Englishe shippe appointed warrlyke belonging to Syr Walter Rawleigh' had been privately funded by a number of Bristol merchants in search of quick profits and not fussy how they were obtained. Representatives of the French owners came over with the backing of the French king and strongly protested about this blatant piracy, but did not get either their ship or their cargo back. Another French vessel was forced to shelter at Uphill in 1652 after crossing from Ireland.

Before coal traffic came to dominate the Uphill arrivals in the nineteenth century there was a regular seasonal trade in the movement of livestock dating back at least to the seventeenth century. The damp, low-lying grassland around Uphill was not suitable for cereal crops but ideal for fattening livestock. Oxen and cows arrived in the months from March to October and were fattened on the lush coastal marshes before being driven to Bristol and other markets, some as far away as London, for slaughter and consumption. Loads of sheep arrived in the months from January to March and were used to restock the herds on higher grounds. Some loads came from Ireland and there were regular arrivals from Sully in South Glamorgan, with three 20-ton vessels bringing over a steady stream of sheep for the grazing lands of Wiltshire and Dorset and of cattle for fattening prior to sale in the Bristol markets. They also brought in pigs sometimes, as well as small quantities of Welsh woollens, and most vessels took produce back with them on the return voyage.

Customs men – riding officers, surveyors and land waiters among them – lived in the small Uphill village, along with seamen and pilots, and at one period a revenue cutter was based in the pill. Many other residents had links with the tiny harbour from the coal merchants and local farmers to the quarrymen and brick workers whose output was loaded away from there. The core coal and cattle business was supplemented by occasional luxury goods from Europe and Ireland, transhipped from deep sea vessels. By the nineteenth century some 16,000 tons of coal and culm were being brought in annually, some for local sale and some to feed the busy limekilns nearby. With salt and timber it largely displaced the old livestock business. Stone from the quarry went in quantity back to Wales and for Somerset sea walls, with fish, salt, cheese and bricks, other important traffics, also being stored and handled.

Uphill was not easy of access. With the help of the tide and the right wind from the west or south-west the approach was relatively straightforward, but other wind conditions might mean having to warp an arriving vessel along the main river and all the way up the pill. Unless there were three men, one had to alternate between the winch and the tiller. When the wind was off the Axe, the vessel entry would be stern first using the anchor as a drogue and dragging a variable length of chain for control, a process known as 'drudging'.

The Enclosure Act of 1813 led to the addition of a public wharf to the previous assorted landing areas. Despite the difficulties of water access, larger vessels began to arrive and their cargoes fed not only the immediate vicinity, but also the growing settlement at neighbouring Weston-super-Mare. There were occasional excursion tug and steamer visits and all sorts of ideas for expansion, including a cross-channel link to Wales. Even without these the Uphill Wharf was a busy little place where Gould's Wharf and Harbour advertised that 'vessels arrive with Welsh and Forest coal every Spring Tide'. There were salt and timber stores too, with the equally busy quarry, kilns and brickworks just a short distance away.

At least one small vessel was built at Uphill, the 18-ton sloop *Hope*, launched in 1802. Eventually, however, the many years of activity ended, the quarry and brickworks closed and the growth of rail and then road transport reduced Uphill to leisure boating use and the adjacent beach to a last resting place for hulks.

Now a quiet haven for small craft, this small pill at Uphill was once busy with coal boats arriving and loads of stone and bricks being dispatched.

Along the main course of the River Axe a wharf at Lympsham dealt mainly with coal for the adjacent farms and local sales, although some vessels were fortunate enough to obtain an outward load of locally-quarried stone. In later years a small Dutch steamer brought in chippings for use on the local roads. The last ketch to bring its cargo of coal up the difficult river approach was the *St Austell*. Skippered by Captain R.V. Hocking, she marked the end of the tradition of manual unloading by basket and winch and for delivery in the locality at 9*d* or 10*d* a hundredweight.

Prior to the building of the sluice at Bleadon and the 1841 opening of the Bristol–Taunton railway line, some upriver movements also went further on, again with cargoes mainly of Welsh or Dean coal.

7. THE PARRETT ESTUARY

The shipping profile of the Somerset coastline from Brean to Stert Island is a fascinating one. The long sandy strand through Berrow to Burnham-on-Sea, now the domain of holiday accommodation and entertainment, saw the occasional cargo landed for the inland villages and, probably, a few illicit arrivals as well.

At Burnham itself Irish cattle boats used to call at the long causeway wharf built primarily for vessels from South Wales, but in-bound traffic there mainly comprised the excursion steamers since the freight arrivals of coal, rails, timber and the like went a short way up the River Brue to the railway wharf at Highbridge. Supplies of fuel and rails for the owning Somerset & Dorset Railway and the lines with which it was associated or connected came in this way in considerable quantity.

Off the entrance to the River Parrett the tidal range can be as much as 40ft on spring tides, half that on neaps. This is among the highest variations in the world and limits access upriver to some twenty days a month for vessels drawing up to 10ft and to ten days for those with a deeper draught, up to 15ft. On the plus side, the strength of the tides helps to keep the river scoured, but variations in tide strength, the amount of rainfall and other variables result in a constantly changing channel along its lower course. When tides are high the best channel is normally the floodway and when they are low the ebbway offers the greatest depth.

Despite the millions of tons of mud in Bridgwater Bay there is full shipping access to the Parrett Estuary via an inward course south of Gore Buoy and north of Stert Island. The outwards channel takes a more northerly course after rounding Stert. A pilot needs to be taken aboard off Burnham, except in the case of small regular visitors, newcomer vessels being guided to the boarding point by VHF radio.

Upstream along the Parrett, Combwich retains the roll-on roll-off facility built to handle materials brought in for building the Hinkley nuclear power station, but bricks and produce are no longer loaded in the pill, nor loads transferred to barges for the hobblers or tugs to tow onwards. Some 8 miles along comes Dunball Wharf, notable as the last of Somerset's traditional harbours to survive. In recent

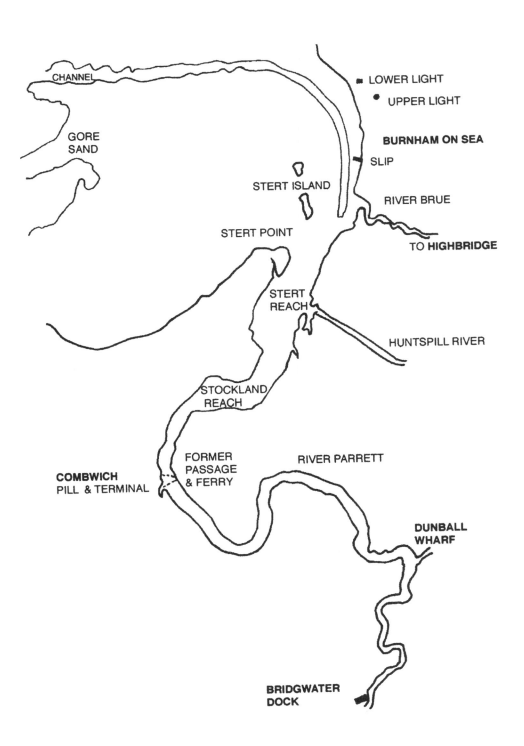

years up to seventy cargoes of sand from Bridgwater Bay sites like Culver Sands have been received annually at the sand wharf adjoining the former railway quays. From the 1990s modern-generation vessels of up to 225ft were still berthing there to discharge their sand.

A more intimate view of the port of Bridgwater can be found in the letters of Captain Norman Curnow who left the sea to become the harbour master there in 1953. Looking back on the thirty-five years before his last pilotage job, Captain Curnow described the activity in the Parrett harbours in a letter he wrote from New Zealand in 2000:

> I came to Bridgwater from sea work in 1953 and I was working there until 1988. Between 1960 and 1980 the port was very busy indeed. There were six working wharves, namely Combwich Wharf, Walpole Wharf (British Petroleum), Bibby's Wharf, Dunball Wharf, Bristol Road Wharf (later Silvey's) and Bridgwater Docks. There were around 3,000 ships per year and we had six pilots.
>
> When I came to Bridgwater there were several schooners still at work e.g. *Result*, *Agnes*, *Emily Barrett*, *Kathleen & May*, *J. T. & S.* (an Irish vessel whose initials stood for John Tyrell & Son of Arklow, predecessor of Arklow Shipping run by Sheila Tyrell).
>
> Dunball supplied coal to R.O.F. (Royal Ordnance Factory) by rail. Ships on that trade were *Roma* and *Radstock* (Captain Holder). Trade to Dunball picked up when the main docks closed. Bridgwater Port & Navigation Authority made a bid for Dunball Wharf but it fell into private hands, Bridgwater Warehousing, Ashmeads of Bristol and later Watts & Co.
>
> Dunball Wharf exported scrap metal (Coopers Metals of Swindon) and imported sand (ARC), fish meal, timber, rock asphalt (Sete), rock salt (Carrickfergus), fertiliser, animal feeds, coal, cement from Poland, Nestles milk from Londonderry.
>
> There were 100 tankers a month to Walpole and every nut and bolt for Hinkley 'A' came by sea on Gardener's ships and Holdersmith to Combwich Wharf. The size of ships averaged 700 tons deadweight.

Bridgwater itself was, of course, the original and most important hub of Parrett shipping despite the access limitations, eased somewhat once steam tugs appeared. It was a greatly varied and busy port and, like Dunball, had rail access for the onward movement of cargoes. Prior to the railway age it was a major transhipment point for goods barged inland along the Parrett to Langport and along the rivers Yeo and Isle tributaries and the Westport Canal. This was the feeder route for a whole network of inland distribution, especially from Langport, just as the Tone Navigation and then the Bridgwater & Taunton Canal fed Taunton and its surrounding areas.

Burnham-on-Sea

Such maritime activity as took place at Burnham before the nineteenth century was almost entirely confined to the small fishing vessels working off its smooth sands and in the waters of Bridgwater Bay. The railway era, coupled with the aspirations of local developers, was to change all that.

No sooner had the Somerset Central Railway taken over the route of the moribund Glastonbury Canal and opened its line to Highbridge in 1854 than it was experimenting with a ferry service across the Bristol Channel to Cardiff. Suitable though a railway wharf at Highbridge might be for freight traffic, a passenger ferry service would be better from Burnham and would save the awkward section up the River Brue to Highbridge. And so an extension of the line was sanctioned in 1855 and three years later a long access pier stretching out from the front at Burnham was opened, much to the chagrin of Bridgwater which had strongly opposed the idea.

Although referred to as a pier, the new structure was just a simple 900ft causeway protruding from the esplanade and sloping down at 1 in 4 to the water. It was linked to the nearby station by a single line whose metals were extended to and across the esplanade and along the pier itself. While the underlying concept remained that of dealing with freight at Highbridge and passengers at Burnham, the station–pier rail line at the latter point was intended to permit the movement of wagons to shipside if needed and might also have been intended for a more comprehensive transfer link with the station.

The passenger ferry service between Burnham and Cardiff began with a sailing of the 121-ton *Iron Duke* on 3 May 1858. She arrived at 10 a.m. with a load of passengers from Cardiff and they were followed by several hundred from Bristol. The Cardiff visitors had a difficult job when it came to board for the return trip as the tide had receded. This highlighted the new pier's berthing problems which the creation of the railway-associated Burnham Tidal Harbour Company was intended to resolve. To limit the considerable effect of the tidal variations at Burnham a channel was dug along one side of the pier, with a wooden mooring structure along its outer side. An adjacent sluicing pond helped to clear away silt, along with a little help from mud scrapers, both afloat and on foot. This done, and using a permutation of four vessels of its own, the BTH reinvigorated the steamer service from 1860.

By 1863 negotiations had led to the newly-formed Somerset & Dorset Railway becoming part of a route link-up which would permit the introduction of a Cardiff–Burnham–Poole–Cherbourg–Paris service. This began in May 1865, but less than two years later S&D financial problems led to the cessation of this facility although the service across to Cardiff continued until 1888.

With no facilities other than its inlaid rail track the pier at Burnham was not really suitable for non-passenger business and lowering and raising wagons

The 'pier' at Burnham-on-Sea with a paddle steamer arriving in the deep channel ready to take on board a quite considerable crowd of excursionists. Nearby small fishing vessels are going about their daily business.

along the 1 in 4 slope would have been a cumbersome process. The odd load of building materials for local use did come ashore, as did some livestock from the periodic Irish cattle boats, the beasts occasionally escaping and causing some hectic moments.

Burnham occupied a strategic position overlooking the access to the Brue and Parrett rivers and early visitors would have seen a succession of vessels entering or leaving those waterways or at anchor waiting for the tide. There was a harbour master's office on the seafront and this was also the base for the river pilots. The town had a lifeboat from 1836, the gift of Sir Peregrine Acland who had his own connection with the sea in the harbour built at Lilstock. The variety of shipping off Burnham can be gauged from the record of rescues embracing four schooners, three barques and a barquentine, four ketches, two trows, a sloop and a smack.

Over the years there have been no less than three lighthouses at Burnham, all still to be seen. Entrepreneurial clergyman Rev. David Davies built the first to

The Low Light, Burnham's second lighthouse, was a simple affair erected on the wide sands to the north of the town. (Roy Gallop)

replace the age-old practice of exhibiting a lantern on the church tower to guide shipping off Stert Point, a service for which shipmasters paid a small fee. The Davies lighthouse was sold to Trinity House for a substantial sum and replaced first by the Low Light on the sands north of the town and then by a traditional building further inland.

Highbridge

For the small Highbridge community the nineteenth century immediately brought change. At one time the River Brue had been one of the water access routes for supplying Glastonbury Abbey and small craft had used the river to trade up to the bridge that crossed it as part of the road link between Bristol and Exeter, but such movements and those further inland were few, small and irregular. New drainage legislation, which first prompted plans for a new wharf for the town, isolated a short section of the old river through the town, but this got a new lease of life as the site chosen by the Glastonbury Canal for a sea lock outlet to the estuary. Opened in 1833 the canal did not last very long and after the canal's demise and replacement by the Somerset Central Railway, the seaward section of the old river beyond the sea lock was seen as the right location for the new railway's ambitions to develop seaborne traffic to feed its metals.

Opening of the SCR line in 1854 was followed by the purchase of land to permit development of the riverside beyond its station. This was reached by an extension which crossed the Bristol & Exeter Railway's main line on the level and then passed over the main Exeter road. The new dock was provided with wharf and unloading facilities which were extended as available finance permitted. Good use was made of these ship–rail transfer facilities and passenger traffic also increased when the railway was extended to Burnham in 1857. Five years later the Somerset Central merged with the Dorset Central Railway to form the Somerset & Dorset Joint company.

With use of the wharf proving rather more profitable than the rest of the railway business, the original wharf area was added to and rail siding arrangements made with a number of businesses which were established in the triangle between the wharfside lines and the passenger line of the 1858 railway extension to Burnham. Highbridge Wharf was well provided with moveable steam cranes which ran on broad gauge tracks, but there were ongoing problems with silting caused by eddying where the old route of the Brue and the new cut joined downstream of the wharf. Special mud clearing operations were required from time to time

Highbridge Wharf.

Highbridge Wharf pictured in late Victorian years. At the head of the line of vessels are two schooners, high in the water having unloaded their cargoes, probably of Scandinavian timber. Beyond are several trows engaged in more local activities.

and there were several cases of vessels having to be diverted because of access difficulties.

With its locomotive and carriage works located on land on the inland side of the station the S&D railway had its own demand for steel and coal. The railway fleet of passenger and cargo vessels was initiated with the iron paddle steamer *Ruby* in 1860, but neither she nor her immediate successors lasted very long. Then, in 1873, the S&D purchased three wooden ketches for cargo carrying, the 59-ton *Railway*, the 69-ton *Julia* and the slightly larger 82-ton *Richard and Emily*. Thirteen years later, two of these were lost at sea, but *Julia* remained active until 1904 when she was replaced by another *Julia* which continued at work until the end of 1933. Locomotive coal was brought over from South Wales and other shipments from there and from the Forest of Dean arrived for local use or onward movement by train. Rails were shipped in, not only for the Highbridge Works and local track use, but also for onward transfer to the London & South Western Railway. Curiously, at one time the locomotive superintendent was also responsible for the S&D vessels.

The iron screw vessel *Alpha* was added to the S&D fleet in 1879 and at one period was coming across from South Wales with a load of rails every two or three days. With the trend for track lengths used on the railway system to increase, she was twice lengthened to carry longer rails; in 1884 and then again in 1905. From 1904 the second *Julia* shared the workload and the 190-ton *Radstock* was added in 1925, the year *Alpha* was finally scrapped.

Timber was another of the staple traffics at Highbridge Wharf, arriving from Scandinavia and Russia for the adjacent John Bland's timber yard and sawmills right until the end of the shipping activity. Loads of grain and flour also arrived while in the outward direction bricks were dispatched from the local brickyard, also some cargoes of local produce and livestock, but inwards movements predominated and outwards sailings of the railway's own ships were usually made in ballast. In the 1920s private sidings served the timber yard, a coal depot, cake mills and a fuel depot.

Trade at Highbridge Wharf suffered a little with the rest of the coasting business when the Severn Tunnel opened, but remained very significant until the period of depression after the First World War. It picked up a little before the 1926 strike period and, like other harbours, Highbridge had a busy time during the second conflict, notably for the storage of war materials for the US Army. But then came another downturn and the end of shipping movements in 1948, with formal closure of the main and new wharves in the following year. Some local rail traffic lingered on for another few years with official closure of the railway to the wharf area in 1965. By the 1970s all the buildings had been abandoned although Highbridge retained its age-old link with the sea through the small boatyard established in 1927 by H.J. Kimber at the Clyce Wharf.

The considerable extent of the S&D Highbridge Wharf is apparent from this view from a vessel discharging timber at the seaward end of the harbour.

The Highbridge boatyard pictured in 1998 and located where the original course of the River Brue joined the later channel.

Dunball

The lower River Parrett through Dunball has been used by shipping since the time of Christ. Danish and other marauders sailed along its lower reaches, pilgrims made it part of their route to Glastonbury and the Romans had settlements with water access there. At Downend the remains of a Norman motte and bailey guarded the river approaches from slightly higher ground and a small port probably existed there for a time.

For centuries little then happened beyond the normal activities of a rural community, apart from a river realignment to reclaim some land in 1677. But all that changed with the opening of the Bristol & Exeter Railway's line to Bridgwater in 1841. The excavations for the new line excited false hopes of coal deposits but, instead, the availability of limestone and the close proximity of the river led to the establishment of lime and cement works, with a tramway to feed them with Welsh and Dean coal discharged at a wharf on the river bank. By 1850 Dunball had three cement and lime factories, two producing bricks and tiles and a manure works. Just beyond the railway lay the supplying quarries.

By an Act of 1867 the main-line railway was authorised to acquire the 1844 tramway to the wharf from its original coal merchant builders, themselves Bristol & Exeter directors. The much-improved connection was opened two years later and the wharf itself subsequently extended. This was a busy period, with the wharf often receiving as many as four vessels at the same time and handling about 100,000 tons of ship cargo a year, mainly of inwards coal and timber. A daily train, broad gauge until the 36-chain branch from the main line was converted to standard in 1892, took coal on to Exeter. The wharf itself had sidings, cranes and stables for the horses which made local deliveries. There was also a 'mudders' hut' for the men who raked the quayside mud out into midstream to provide a flat bottom for visiting vessels, with the tide then clearing the mud away. Across the main road the Greenhill Arms, named after the lord of the manor, provided refreshment for men from the vessels, works and railway.

The beginning of the twentieth century was a busy time for Dunball. In the half year from May to November 1905, 198 vessels were dealt with representing a total of 10,906 tons and an average of 55.8 tons per vessel. For the same period eight years later, with Britain now on the brink of war, the number had dropped to seventy-five vessels and the tonnage to 4,258. The pattern over the months of the year did not vary greatly, although December was usually less busy. One of the larger visitors was the 68-ton *Champion*, which arrived five times in April 1913 and thirty-six times in the year as a whole. The smallest was little *Lily*, just 25 tons, which called once. She had been built at Penrhyn in 1897 and had had several owners before being bought by A. Oxenham of Lynmouth.

Motorised in 1927, she was the ubiquitous little vessel which foundered off the Usk two years later while heading across the Bristol Channel with a load of coal for her Weston, Clevedon & Portishead Railway owners.

Elsewhere details are shown of the vessels using Dunball in 1904 – some twenty-six being berthed there at one time or another during the year and these making thirty-eight arrivals in the December. Ketches and other sailing vessels predominated, but had already been joined by small steamers. The proportion of the latter increased after the First World War until it reached two-thirds, although the tonnage handled slowly and steadily declined. Even so the location remained important, not least because of the advantage it had always enjoyed of having a greater depth than the upstream section on to Bridgwater and the fact that it could often be used when higher parts of the river were frozen over.

In the second half of the twentieth century Dunball changed completely when the M5 motorway was driven through the cement works area on the inland side of the station. The old works disappeared one after another and then the

A crane stands waiting for the *Mary-C* to moor up at Dunball Wharf in July 1999. Beyond is the former Bibby's wharf and plant.

wharf lost its rail link in 1962. Even so the shipping activity continued, now with modern vessels and large bulk cargoes. Not far from the former railway wharf Shell-Mex and BP added a fuel storage and delivery depot in 1953 with Bibby's animal feed site adding to the coal and timber still arriving at the original location. Channel-dredged sand and gravel came in to a separate wharf site near the end of the King's Sedgemoor Drain, with the wharf proper still being used by modern motor vessels which would have dwarfed the trows and ketches that once were the location's regulars.

Although the Walpole oil terminal, just downstream from the original wharf, closed in 1987, Dunball was still active twenty years later, making it Somerset's last surviving port. It could take much larger vessels, although these needed some 10ft of water, which occurred every seven or eight days. They would wait at Gore Buoy off Burnham until about two-and-a-half hours before high water and arrive at Dunball just before the flood had topped, turning with their bows into the river bend so that the tide could ease them against the wharf, in exactly the same manner as their sailing vessel predecessors. Later cargoes were mainly animal feed in bulk for Bibby's, Portuguese granite sets for road-making purposes and rock salt from Northern Ireland. A.G. Watts operated the wharf, acted as shipping agents, and provided road transport. ARC (Southern) Ltd brought in self-discharge sand aggregate boats to the separate stacking area by the wharf.

The two motor vessels *Balmoral* and *Oldenberg* even made occasional excursion visits and moored exactly where the old wooden *Champion* had appeared so often with its cargo of coal from Penarth or Cardiff.

Bridgwater

Bridgwater has a long history as a settlement and an early harbour. It derived its origins from its location as a place where the River Parrett narrowed sufficiently to be crossed, but would later suffer because its waterway access involved a winding approach along 14 miles of the river and was subject to the limitations imposed by its varying tidal depths. The town's history as a port falls into several fairly distinct periods. From the limited, small vessel activities of the early years, ship arrivals and departures accelerated in the seventeenth and eighteenth centuries, rose to a peak around 1880 and then began a slow decline to the First World War and a rapid one thereafter.

Early charters and other documents confirm shipping activity at Bridgwater at least as early as 1200 when the first bridge was built, and the town was soon to feature in the growing national practice of hiring or requisitioning vessels when needed to transport troops and supplies to various conflicts. By the end of the century Bridgwater vessels were involved in carrying supplies to support military adventures on the Continent, and from 1314 were doing the same service to aid the monarch's quarrels with the Scots. But trade and commerce is never to be denied and it can be glimpsed by the existence, a few years earlier, of records of a load of lead going to Gascony in the vessel *Sauneye*. By the end of the century commercial activity was such that the primitive early harbour facilities needed improvement to cater for the substantial volume of local produce then being sent to Ireland, France and Spain and to aid the unloading of the wine, hides, twine, hemp and esparto grass being imported in the reverse direction.

Such was the growth in the fourteenth century that in 1348 Bridgwater was freed from the shackles of Bristol to become a fiscal port in its own right, controlling the harbours along 80 miles of Somerset coast from the Axe to the Devon border, together with an outbase, curiously, on the Mumbles in South Wales. The Langport Slip, just upstream of Bridgwater's Town Bridge, was built in 1488, reinforcing the importance of the town as a transhipment point for inland movements. Cloth was a major shipping export cargo in the fifteenth and sixteenth centuries but, starting in the latter, a period of decline began which had dropped the number of Bridgwater registered vessels to just seven in 1592 and only one in 1596. It was to be another hundred years before trade really picked up again. When it did, commodities like coal and salt grew to quite significant tonnages.

Small vessels predominated in the eighteenth century, sloops, smacks and trows, with the number of vessels owned locally rising by an average of one a year from the thirty-three of 1786 and peaking at around 150 a hundred years later. The volume of inland movement grew in parallel, as did the size of commercial operators. The Bobbett family, for example, owned trows to bring coal over from Wales, lighters to take it forward after transhipment at Bridgwater and packhorses to get it to its final destination. Even places like Wellington now had access to cheaper, albeit not yet cheap, coal supplies.

The Bobbett era was followed by that of Stuckey & Bagehot, whose fleet grew out of an initial small number of barges used to move salt and other commodities from Bridgwater to their quayside storage and distribution point at Langport. From this followed the use of coasters to bring supplies into Bridgwater and then a fleet of deep-sea ships sailing as far as the North American mainland and even India. By the mid-1830s they owned and operated around thirty-five vessels. Timber was one of the principal imports with the larger vessels discharging to lighter at Combwich which was less restricted of access than Bridgwater itself, being that much nearer the Bristol Channel. Other large shipowners later included Sully's which operated and chartered a large fleet, but majored on the coal trade with their own stacking ground beside the inner harbour and a network of factors for finding trows and ketches for their shipments from Lydney, Newport, Cardiff and Swansea.

The Bridgwater wharves were busy places at the beginning of the nineteenth century, not only with the vessels themselves, but with all the people, trades and infrastructure associated with a port. Like the rest of the country, the end of the long wars with France slowly prompted a dramatic rise in trade and commerce and by the 1820s Bridgwater shipping trade was increasing at something like 5,000 tons a year. Plans to bypass part of the downstream section of the Parrett foundered, but a better link to Taunton was achieved in 1827 when the Bridgwater & Taunton Canal was opened to link the county town with Huntworth on the stretch of the Parrett just beyond Bridgwater's Town Bridge.

More and more South Wales coal began to come in from Cardiff and Newport, along with Forest of Dean coal from Lydney, as the output of the collieries served by those places expanded. Lower grade fuel like culm came in from Swansea, and there was a wide range of general cargoes coming into Bridgwater, among which oats, slates and salt featured prominently. Livestock, Irish linen, timber and a host of other commodities all helped to create an immense variety of goods and the services and facilities for dealing with them. The riverside wharves could not cope with all the extra business on offer and the harbour authority, the Town Corporation, had to do something.

Pressure on the Bridgwater & Taunton Canal Company led the latter to seek and obtain parliamentary approval in 1837 for an extension of the canal from Huntworth to a new dock on the seaward side of Bridgwater and a lock to connect with the River Parrett there. The move complimented the Parrett Navigation Act of the previous year so that when the new dock opened in 1841, the onward links to Taunton and Langport had also increased their capacity. Not only this, but in the same year the Bristol & Exeter Railway reached Bridgwater from the Bristol end, something which subsequently proved a mixed blessing, for while the docks were to be linked with the main line by an 1846 railway connection, the railway took so much business away from the canal that it headed steadily towards receivership. Despite this the port proper continued to expand its business with the coal and other inwards movements supplemented by more outwards flows which were dominated by bricks and tiles, often for Irish and the more distant domestic locations. The traditional business of local and inland distributing continued.

With its large agricultural hinterland Bridgwater was the natural outlet for local produce and an important staging point for the supply of a variety of incoming general cargoes, ranging from wines and spirits to exotic spices from faraway places. These longer distance imports brought larger vessels into Bridgwater and ocean-going schooners, barques and brigs were a regular sight. Small vessel traffic included trows from Gloucester and the Middle Severn, and before the Bristol & Exeter Railway's arrival in 1841 there were regular market boats and passenger packets to Bristol and even London.

Until that momentous year of 1841 all shipping had to sit on the mud beside the wharves of the main river to load or discharge their cargoes. Downstream of the Town Bridge the East and West quays would be lined with vessels, all having to be managed in varying water depths, mindful of the regular 2ft bore wave along the river and even wary of being frozen in from time to time by a bout of low temperatures. Upstream of the bridge was the mooring place for barges, either waiting to go alongside for transhipment or handling their cargoes over the Langport Slip. The dry dock and shipyard was on the East Quay side and the Custom House on the West.

The 1841 opening of the new dock was an occasion of great celebration as the pioneer wooden paddle tug *Endeavour* took its party of honoured guests to bring in the sloop *Henry* to accord it the distinction of being the first sailing vessel to enter the dock. Vessels of up to 180ft in length and 30ft beam could be accommodated but, even so, insufficient river depth during and around neap tides meant several days when the new wharf at Dunball had to be used instead. The same year had other significances, one of which was the opening of the Taff Vale Railway to carry coal from colliery to the sea at Penarth. From this beginning would stem the Marquess of Bute's dock building at Cardiff and later, as the demand for coal went on increasing, the new docks at Barry. In 1845 the status of the Port of Bridgwater changed slightly by virtue of an Act of Parliament which defined its area as that from Brean Down to Hinkley Point.

Another significant but less celebrated milestone occurred in 1864 when the UK Telegraph Company opened an office in Bridgwater. Now owners, captains and agents could communicate quickly at just a shilling for twenty words. This made the linking of vessels and loads so much easier than the previous reliance on the post, and the rise in business continued. From an annual tonnage level of around 75,000 tons in 1822, the total handled by the wider port had risen to 261,282 tons by 1880, 3,677 vessels being involved. Inwards coal still predominated, but at least twenty other commodities arrived in significant quantities, especially grain. These were the busiest years for Bridgwater with the steam tugs, barges, dock workers, chandlers, repairers and other shore-based activities at full stretch.

The shipping activity at Bridgwater stretched for some 2 miles along the River Parrett. From Chilton Trinity on the downstream approaches to the town and the site of a busy brickworks, it continued past the S&D railway wharf, the dock entrance and the first silt slime batches of the Bath Brick industry. Then came the crowded wharf areas of the East and West quays before the river passed under the Town Bridge and by the Langport Slip and the barge mooring area to then reach the final group of slime batches. Altogether it was a busy, colourful and productive hive of maritime business.

From 1876 the dock was acquired by the Great Western Railway as a result of the Bristol & Exeter's 1867 purchase of the Bridgwater & Taunton Canal, and it was provided with rail siding access crossing the river by means of a novel steam-operated bridge in which a section of rail moved sideways to allow the bridge

Bridgwater Dock seen from the entrance lock and looking towards the inner basin and main dock. On the left is a collier adjacent to Sully's coal stacking ground, with the dock warehouse beyond.

section to be retracted. The dock now began to take on its final form with the British Oil & Cake Mills, opened in 1869, on one side and a large warehouse on the other. Sully & Co. occupied the stacking ground beside the inner dock. Both dock and river had cranage facilities and the Somerset & Dorset Railway's 1890 branch line from Edington Junction had its own wharf on the east bank of the river.

In this heyday the two paddle tugs *Petrel* and *Victor* were kept busy despite the appearance of steam coasters, but the good times were not to last and a double blow fell upon the port in 1886. A major work to remove a great volume of mud from the dock and canal kept the port access limited for some six weeks, just at a time when the Great Western Railway opened its Severn Tunnel link from South Wales into Gloucestershire. Prior to this the rail movement of coal to Somerset involved a circuitous journey via Gloucester and Bristol, but now the route mileage involved in a rail journey was greatly reduced. Additionally, some shippers could not afford to retard their business while the port reopened and others found the railway rates more attractive and the train services more reliable than the traditional terms sailing vessel owners could offer. The number of vessels using Bridgwater dropped by some 30 per cent, with a similar decline in the business tonnage previously handled each year.

Although the size of sailing vessels using Bridgwater increased slowly within the port's overall dimension restrictions, a surprising number were still small, the size range varying from 20 to 450 tons. Steamers were now appearing more often and accounted for 16 per cent of the number of vessels entering the docks in the early 1880s. Journeys, destinations and commodities were getting more

Viewed from the entrance from the River Parrett, the dock at Bridgwater is nearing the end of its working life, but still accommodates a fair-sized motor vessel. One of the sluices is visible to the left of the entrance lock.

varied. Coal in and bricks out – both the building and the Bath Brick scouring variety – remained the staples throughout, but outwards movements, formerly concentrated on the local coasts and across to Ireland, now often embraced the Mediterranean, Scandinavia – a good source of timber return loads – and Atlantic Europe, as well as London, Scotland and the East Coast of Britain.

Traffic on the Bridgwater & Taunton Canal ended around 1906 and five years later the inland Parrett trade was virtually ended when a barge laden with bricks sank on the upstream side of the Town Bridge. However, as elsewhere, the sail, motorised and steam shipping using the port of Bridgwater still remained significant until the First World War although the shipbuilding activity at Carver's yard just downstream of the East Quay and the modest dry dock had begun to peter out before the end of the nineteenth century. The ketch *Irene* was built there as late as 1907 and the services of surveying, repair and fitting out continued. But the port had silting problems; the ubiquitous railways ran everywhere and initially used the emerging lorry culture to expand their penetration by operating road collection and delivery services. Road transport was then to become pre-eminent in its own right, facilitating the demand for the immediacy benefits provided by smaller loads and quicker transits.

The launch of the *Irene* marked the beginning of the end for Bridgwater's shipbuilding activity. It had seen some notable achievements, not least the building of a schooner, the *Ellen*, achieved by Prosser virtually single-handed, rigging, ironwork and all. Altogether it has been calculated that some 167 ships were built in the town, not counting the many rowing and other small boats. The busiest period had been in the nineteenth century and, although the East Quay dry dock continued in use for repairs well into the twentieth, it provided its last service for a coaster surveyed there in 1940. Business activity and employment in Bridgwater was, in its shipping heyday, dominated by the seafaring trade, not just that of the dock warehouse, the railway wharves, coal and timber stacking and the huge Bath Brick loadings, but also by the daily activities of the chandlers, provision suppliers, bankers and the Customs House men on the West Quay.

By the middle of the twentieth century outwards shipping traffic consisted almost entirely of bricks and inwards sand, coal and timber, most of it through the Dunball satellite. The end of an era was signalled in 1963 with an announcement by British Rail that it would close Bridgwater Dock if it could find no buyers for it. This began a long period of discussion and stagnation followed by the eventual rehabilitation of the canal, the creation of a small marina in the former ship dock area and the conversion of the dockside there to modern housing.

The following tonnage, shipping and event list gives some idea of the fortunes of Bridgwater over the busiest period of its long history as an important port:

Bridgwater Dock in 1999 with the old warehouse converted to dwellings and new buildings added around the main marina water area. An old crane has been retained with chains and an anchor by its base.

1822	Shipping trade of around 75,000 tons annually
1827	Bridgwater & Taunton Canal opened to Huntworth
1829	Shipping trade now 112,000 tons annually
1840	First steam tug into service
1841	Canal extended and enclosed dock opened; Bristol & Exeter Railway arrives
1851	First excursion by steam tug
1855	2,314 vessels, 112,395 tons **(a)**
1856	2,281 vessels, 110,994 tons – average 48.6 tons
1878	3,864 vessels, 233,039 tons – average 60.3 tons
1879	4,089 vessels, 243,915 tons – average 59.6 tons

1880	3,677 vessels, 216,282 tons – average	58.8 tons
1886	Severn Tunnel opened shortening rail journeys	
1891	2,648 vessels, 166,768 tons – average	62.9 tons
1893	2,373 vessels, 149,282 tons – average	62.9 tons
1903	2,975 vessels, 163,960 tons – average	55.1 tons
1912	1,586 vessels, 105,972 tons – average	66.8 tons
1913	1,588 vessels, 104,512 tons – average	67.1 tons
1933	817 vessels, 74,664 tons – average	91.4 tons
1953	527 vessels, 52,776 tons – average	100.1 tons
1972	667 vessels, 582,636 tons – average	873.5 tons **(b)**
1981	432 vessels, 440,329 tons – average	1019.3 tons **(b)**

(a) **[Despite the Parrett being frozen for a long period which reduced seamen to begging in the streets of the town]**

(b) **[Made up of modern motor vessels at Dunball Wharf]**

Combwich

Shipping activity began at Combwich sometime in the fourteenth century and, as far back as 1480, the *Anne* carrying cork, hides and fish on the Minehead–Bristol run called there, and corn was being exported. In later years Irish and other ships called regularly with coal, wine, iron, millstones, beans and oil. Salt was unloaded at Combwich for weighing and storage before being moved on to Bridgwater and a ship was built there in the 1690s. All this in a tiny creek, which was nevertheless the site of the first harbour and settlement along the course of the River Parrett. A ridge of hard rock formed a shallow 'passage' across the river which could be used by livestock and horse-drawn vehicles at low tide, and for centuries a ferry plied between the village on the south bank and the track to Pawlett on the other.

In the eighteenth century coal and culm was being unloaded at a wharf in the pill and the shipping trade increased. Henry Leigh built up the harbour facilities and Henry Leigh the younger exported bricks and tiles from his yard south of the pill. The output of the two local tile- and brickworks became the main trade with sailings to Bristol, to Ireland, the South Wales ports and up the Severn. By the 1890s vessels were going as far as Sharpness and Bideford. Coal was the main return load, especially for the brickworks.

The vessels ranged from small cutters, sometimes part-owned by local farmers, to 400-ton ships. In addition to those lying in the pill, others were unloaded at moorings in Combwich Reach and their cargoes lightered up the Parrett to Bridgwater and beyond. The larger vessels of the Stuckey & Bagehot fleet mainly used Combwich until the dock was built at Bridgwater in 1841. Some

This typical example of an early Bristol Channel buoy now sits in quiet retirement on the edge of the pill at Combwich. Its construction clearly owes much to traditional barrel-making methods.

Low water in the pill at Combwich, once quite a busy little harbour. The relatively modern facility on the right was built to receive construction materials for Hinkley Point nuclear power station.

lightermen and hobblers lived at Combwich and dealt with Canadian timber which was barged or rafted upriver.

There was considerable agricultural trade in the first part of the twentieth century including that of the Combwich & District Farmers Association which owned the ketch *Emily* lost in 1934. Colthurst Symons took over the Leigh brickyard and used the *Irene* to carry the brick output, but the brickyard closed sometime in the 1930s. Then shipping activity petered out and the pill slowly silted up. More recently, there was a short-term new lease of life for Combwich in the late 1950s when CEGB built a modern wharf to handle materials for Hinkley power station. It may again be used for this purpose but, in the meantime, Combwich is just a quiet anchorage for a few small pleasure craft with little evidence of its busy shipping days.

8. WEST SOMERSET

Much of the coast between the Parrett Estuary and the Devon border is quite exposed, with a shingle shoreline and low cliffs. The Brendon, Quantock and Exmoor foothills are gentle pastoral areas, producers of the fruits of agriculture and long-time consumers of coal and culm for the limekilns that fed the soil. Only minor activity took place at Stolford and Kilve – condemned as a dangerous landing place in 1559, but still with the traditional small limekiln burning stone from South Wales – while the purpose-built estate dock at Lilstock had to surrender to storms and the changes of the twentieth century.

The older settlement at Watchet had a port of sorts, battered in its early years by gales and always inferior to Minehead, but coming into prominence with the South Wales demand for Brendon iron ore and later busy with wood pulp for the local papermaking activity. Dunster probably had a small harbour at one time, Blue Anchor beach hosted the occasional ship visitor and Porlock Weir had a contrived but cute little harbour and now hosts a few leisure craft. In between, Minehead has a long history as Somerset's second port, sheltered by North Hill and having an on-going and very varied trade with West Wales, Ireland, Bristol and even deeper waters.

Lilstock
A few modest streams reach Bridgwater Bay in the long coastal stretch between Stert Point and Watchet, but the only working harbour was at Lilstock. Stolford

certainly figured in one of the various channel-to-channel ship canal schemes and Kilve might have been important if a grandiose oil shale speculation had proved viable but, remote as it is, Lilstock actually hosted regular shipping visits for the best part of a century.

Lilstock village, which never had more than a hundred inhabitants, lies a short distance inland, by the side of a small stream that curves around some higher ground to emerge from behind a pebble bank and add its waters to Bridgwater Bay. The shingle area foreshore represented a convenient spot for small sailing vessels to discharge their cargoes of coal and culm for Sir John Acland's estate limekilns and for his home at Fairfield House. The house was only 2 miles away and the estate yielded the occasional return load of pit props for the expanding coal-mining activity across the Bristol Channel.

When Isabel, the daughter of Sir John's son Peregrine, was advised to live by the sea to aid her delicate constitution a small dwelling was built for her on the heights above the stream's final course through the pebble bank. There she could entertain and enjoy the sea air, while on the bank itself a promenade was constructed to accommodate leisure outings in her coach. At the same time, around 1830, an enclosed dock was constructed between the promenade and the heights behind. The waters of the stream were diverted to flow into the dock at

This grassy hollow is the site of the former dock at Lilstock viewed from the turning area at the west end of the site.

the western end and gates and sluices provided at its eastern exit. Local limestone was doubtless used to create the high quality surrounds provided for the dock, and other works from this period included a breakwater and a decent access road.

The waters of the stream enabled the dock to be flushed out as needed and gave a good measure of control over the water level inside. It became increasingly busy with the incoming cargoes of fuel and occasionally other commodities. There was a limekiln up on the heights to the east and a double one behind the dock approaches. This was a period of expansion for village and dock. A few dwellings were built just along from the harbour entrance, coastguards were stationed there from 1848, and then a customs officer from 1855. On occasions there could be up to as many as three vessels in the dock, some able to secure an outward load of estate timber, burnt lime or corn.

Activity at the Lilstock port peaked in the second half of the nineteenth century when the village population reached ninety-four. Around this time also, the Admiralty had some thoughts of a canal link to Seaton, one of the many schemes mooted for linking the Bristol and English channels. The pier had

On the shingle foreshore at Lilstock the outine of the dock entrance quay and breakwater are still visible.

become a fashionable spot, with carriages bringing parties for picnics supplied from a butler's pantry and shelter at the end. Paddle steamers called on the way to and from Burnham, Cardiff and Ilfracombe, bringing Victorian tourists for a brief stay in the pleasant little spot.

The dock activity itself was sufficient to warrant a small warehouse behind the south wall, a building that also served to host special events for the local Lilstock community. Like the village church, the Limpet Shell beerhouse and the quayside houses, it has now gone.

Refreshments could still be obtained from one of the original quayside houses until the last years of the First World War, but by that time declining trade and encroaching shingle, combined with storm damage around the turn of the century, had brought an end to the commercial use of the port. The pier was destroyed after that war and the houses gradually fell into ruins although a lime burner's cottage was still in use in 1932. Another war brought a brief period of coastal use as a bombing range, but now only a few areas of masonry and overgrown limekilns mark what was once a busy little harbour.

Watchet

The Danes wreaked havoc on the small Watchet settlement several times in the tenth century, but its position at the mouth of the Washford River later enabled it to grow as a modest trading place. At this period various quite tiny vessels brought in necessities and took produce outwards, a progression periodically disrupted, however, by the gales to which an exposed location made Watchet vulnerable. Initially that exposed coastal location was shielded by little more than a rough stone breakwater which frequently needed rebuilding owing to storm damage.

Despite its limitations as a harbour, seaborne trade at Watchet dates back to at least 1210 and there were shipping links with Bristol and South Wales in the following two centuries. There were also further destructive storms, but by the sixteenth century cargoes of coal, livestock and provisions were coming in steadily, possibly along with wine and salt from France, and local produce went regularly to Bristol to meet the needs of that city's growing population and importance. The simple pier jetty suffered another round of damage in 1659 and took some time to rebuild. Over these early years the main shipping cargoes were irregular but ongoing, with inward movements of coal, salt, wine and livestock from Channel, Irish and French ports, the coal shipments always predominating.

The former simple jetty was eventually improved after the storm damage of 1659 and soon some 150 vessels were being dealt with annually, a few of them owned by local people. In the second half of the seventeenth century Watchet was the main area port for bringing in Welsh coal, with Minehead occupying that eminence in the livestock activity. There was regular business with Ireland, kelp for Bristol's glass industry was at this period a major export, with coal from

Swansea, Neath and Tenby the major import. A number of seamen lived locally.

Gales brought more damage to Watchet's harbour and trade aspirations in 1701 and again in 1706. As lords of the manor and owners of the port, the Wyndham family invested in rebuilding, giving Watchet a new quay in 1708 and the town and the Wyndhams the benefit of increased trade and port dues. Prompted by wool merchants and their dissatisfaction with the cost of bringing in Irish wool through Minehead, there were hopes that Watchet might become a customs port, but the application to Parliament ran into determined opposition from Minehead interests. Bridgwater, too, objected in order to protect its involvement in the flows of Irish wool moving up the Parrett. Thus no great changes occurred except that the variety of cargoes increased, especially the commodities transhipped from the larger vessels serving Bristol. The range of ports served also widened, but the harbour facilities remained inadequate for any significant expansion in trade and the number of locally owned vessels remained in modest figures.

That is until midway through the nineteenth century when everything was to change. The catalyst was the growing demand for iron, the resultant increase in the needs of the Welsh iron-makers and the transformation of earlier scratching for ore on the Brendon Hills into a serious mining activity. To enable the output to be shipped in bulk over to South Wales, the West Somerset Mineral Railway was formed and opened a line inland from Watchet to Comberow in 1857 and then extended it ¾ mile up a 1 in 4 incline to a summit near Raleigh's Cross on top of the Brendons over the next four years.

Concurrently with this first legislation, another Act of 1857 facilitated the reconstruction of Watchet's harbour, duly completed in 1861–62 to enable it to cater for much larger vessels. In place of the old practice of carting ore down from the mines to load on to vessels beached on the harbour mud, the railway now brought wagons of ore down to a rebuilt West Quay where they could discharge from a projecting jetty directly into ships lying alongside. Conventional railway facilities also arrived in the form of the Bristol & Exeter Railway's line from Taunton which had a connection leading to shipment facilities at the new East Quay.

Watchet became a thriving place with 40,000 tons of ore exported annually at the peak and up to a dozen vessels using the port in some weeks. It was home to twenty-one master mariners along with ten shipowners and several ancillary shipping enterprises. Other trades and activities had expanded with the wealth generated by the iron ore traffic and the first holidaymakers had arrived and demanded accommodation, entertainment and other such facilities, including steamer excursions.

The new prosperity suffered a major setback at the end of the nineteenth century with the Welsh ironworks switching to imported ore, the rundown of

Watchet Harbour pictured a few years after the Second World War and with two vessels lying at the East Quay. The one-time exports of iron ore from the Brendon mines were unloaded from wagon to ship at the West Quay.

the mines leading to their eventual closure in 1883 and then that of the railway in 1898. As if that were not enough, two major storms wreaked havoc on the town and harbour sinking several vessels and damaging others, and attempts to revive the Brendon mining proved unsuccessful.

After a severe gale in December 1900 and more severe weather in 1903, the damaged harbour was rebuilt by the Harbour Board of Commissioners in 1904 at an eventual cost of £25,000. Kelly's Directory then described it in the following terms:

The tidal harbour has an area of 10 acres, and a depth of water at the entrance of 9 feet at low neap tide, and of 22 feet at high water (ordinary spring tides) over a large portion of this area; it is well sheltered from all winds, being protected on the west by the new pier and a breakwater 390 feet in length; and on the north-east by a pier 560 feet in length, which also forms a convenient quay for steamers and coasting vessels; steam cranes are supplied at nominal rates for discharging cargoes; the harbour thus inclosed [*sic*] is lined with substantial quay walls and a landing slip; in its fine seaward approaches, the depth of water at its entrance and its direct railway communication with the interior, Watchet harbour possesses advantages beyond any other small port in the Bristol channel.

In the first part of the twentieth century the port of Watchet depended primarily upon import movements of coal and Scandinavian wood pulp. When the iron ore bonanza ended it had become a much less important harbour than either Bridgwater or Minehead and then shared with them the inexorable move away from short sea movement of goods. Had it not been for the paper mills, coal, pulp and esparto grass it would not have survived. Indeed, for many years the paper mills' small steamer *Rushlight* was a familiar arrival with its regular cargoes of coal, with *Arran Monarch* taking over this mantle and arriving regularly in the 1950s. The mills also used wood pulp from the Gulf of Bothnia and esparto grass from North Africa and some supplies also passed inland for other mills.

Low tide at Watchet Harbour in the 1950s with a collier sitting on the mud and a line of empty railway wagons on the East Quay. (Jane Lily)

There was more damage to Watchet Harbour from a gale-driven high tide at the beginning of 1962, and once again parts of it had to be rebuilt. However, a new era was dawning with the 1966 news that the West Somerset Shipping Company was to lease quay space with every expectation of developing new traffics to supplement the supplies for and products from the still important paper mills along the Washford River. Watchet's seaborne trade did suffer a major setback when the paper mills converted to oil, but, new exports of motor parts and tractors, and later the addition of a small container facility on the East Quay along with warehouses and cranage, kept Watchet busy with a full range of facilities to handle the developing flows of Russian and Scandinavian timber and other cargoes such as wheat, fruit pulp, wines, cork and other general goods.

But Watchet's reborn harbour could not withstand the universal rise of the bigger container ports, the growing size of road vehicles and the pressures on modest-sized industries and activities. Its mercurial links with the sea continued through a period of relative stagnation and the occasional entertainment of teams

The Watchet Harbour workboat-cum-dredger, which appears to be the same vessel that once worked in the Bridgwater waters as the eroder *Perseverance*.

wrestling in the harbour mud, leading eventually to a complete remodelling to harness the harbour waters as a marina for the accommodation of leisure vessels.

Minehead

Centuries ago small local vessels probably worked into and out of the entrance to the modest Pill River which emerges into Blue Anchor Bay at the eastern end of what is now a small holiday area where the Somerset coastline approaches Minehead. The needs and produce of the Old Cleeve and Carhampton areas would not have occasioned more than the odd sailing, however, but there was doubtless some local fishing activity. Nearer Minehead itself, Dunster occupied a much different status as the seat of the powerful de Mohun family, and later of the Luttrells. Its impressive castle needed shipping access and its countless manors needed outlets for their produce. Oddly enough, we know of activity at a harbour at the mouth of the River Avill in 1183 because of a fine levied upon the reeve in connection with corn apparently arriving there illegally.

The Dunster vessel *Mary* was captured by the French in 1375; the port comes to notice again around 1418 and in the following century when wool is arriving from Milford. Vessels to and from Ireland called occasionally in the first half of the seventeenth century but the Luttrells, now in control of local affairs, were already investing in improved shipping facilities at Minehead to cater for increasing trade. There were also problems resulting from the gradual silting up of the tiny Avill affecting its former role as an access route to the castle.

Handy as it would have been to have small vessels coming up the Avill to the site of the mill below the walls of Dunster Castle, and to Gallox Bridge just beyond, there were other considerations for the Luttrell family. Other local trade could yield very useful sums of money from the dues raised on shipping and this would have been a significant factor in leading to the encouragement of more maritime activity through Minehead and in prompting the Luttrell investment in a simple jetty there around 1420. Primary customs income accrued to the Crown, but there were various other charges upon shipping levied for the upkeep of the port and the ancillary services provided and, as always, local people would also have found a variety of other ways to benefit from additional shipping business.

The first move to improve the age-old practice of loading and unloading vessels lying on the mud or shingle would merely have been a string of boulders from local cliffs, dragged into the shallows at low tide and levered into some sort of orderly position. By the end of the fifteenth century, however, this primitive jetty was proving totally inadequate for the growing trade with Ireland, France and across the Bristol Channel. There was more Luttrell funding for major improvements to handle the mainstream movements of livestock, produce, coal and yarn. Keelage charges of the period reveal that Aberthaw boats paid only half the normal 4d per vessel and salt only a quarter.

Under a charter of 1558 Minehead became a borough, but the council failed miserably to adequately maintain the harbour for which they were now responsible. Result, a long round of petition and counter-petition between the Luttrell family and the corporation before its eventual return to the care of the former in 1604 and the construction of a new pier by them, completed in 1616. The century was to be a busy and varied one for maritime Minehead.

A period of prosperity followed the completion of the new harbour with an increase in the traditional movements and in salt and wine as well. Local markets were being stimulated by goods brought over in quantity from the Glamorgan harbours, along with wool arriving to feed the growing activities of Exmoor weavers. The long-standing fishing activity kept expanding and Minehead now sent a fishing fleet to Newfoundland to supplement, and eventually to replace, the long-standing export trade in herrings. Along with Irish livestock, sea coal and the essential salt staple, together with outward cargoes of local produce, Minehead's harbour proved a busy, useful and profitable place. In the 1640s a number of Minehead vessels were also kept busy taking troops and supplies to Ireland and frequently bringing refugees from that torn land on the return sailing.

There were interludes in this bustling peaceful activity when Minehead ships and men embarked upon decidedly dubious commercial enterprises. The town fitted out privateers to seek out French and Spanish victims in the five years of war from 1625 and a number of prizes were brought into the harbour by others operating under Letters of Marque. Similar activities took place in the War of Spanish Succession from 1701 to 1714. By then the status of Minehead had been increased, albeit still under the aegis of Bridgwater, and there had been further harbour improvements in 1682.

Not that Minehead was without its own small local dramas for there was a great deal of smuggling activity in the town. Wine and spirits, cloth, tobacco and a host of other commodities were illicitly whisked ashore to be hidden in the cellars of houses near the harbour and of the older area around the church before being sold to an ever-eager clientele. Even the revenue men themselves occasionally had a hand in the activity.

Some thirty vessels were owned locally at the beginning of the eighteenth century and for some time the trade prosperity continued, helped by more pier extension and re-equipment works. Imports of Irish wool grew steadily, with some forty or so vessels working to and from various Irish ports. By the middle of the century the cloth imports were arriving almost daily to fill the quays and warehouse, with cargoes of yarn, hides, skins and produce also being discharged in quantity. The trade in salted herrings was booming, at one-time reaching a level of some 4,000 barrels a year being moved to Mediterranean ports, and now greatly expanded beyond the regular supplies to Bristol, to travel to destinations not only throughout the Mediterranean but even as far as the West Indies and

South America. The itineraries tended to be triangular with return loads of produce for Bristol and then back to Minehead, often with imports transhipped at Bristol and brought home for local markets. Some imports also arrived after transhipment at Barnstaple.

The fortunes of Minehead's port began to decline as early as the later years of the eighteenth century, the long-distance sailings tapered off, the Newfoundland fish business declined and even the age-old Irish traffic had dropped to warranting only three locally-owned vessels. Gone was the prestigious trade with Virginia and the West Indies and only the coasting business remained substantial. In the nineteenth century Minehead's shipping activity slowed down even further and a note of 1829 reveals only two vessels still working regularly to Bristol and three or four to Wales. Such was the decline that in 1834 the town lost its status as a separate port and reverted to being encompassed in the coastal aegis of Bridgwater. The last vessel registered at Minehead, the sloop *Harriet*, came to a sad end when caught in bad weather while unloading a cargo of limestone from Porthcawl. More positively for the well-being of the town and its commercial activity, the first excursion steamer had arrived in 1824.

Minehead was formerly a busy and important harbour, as shown by this collection of several cutters and two larger vessels, probably ketches, moored alongside one another.

Toward the end of the 1800s the trade activity in Minehead Harbour had declined to but a shadow of its once hectic pace. Holidaymakers were now the income producers and many trippers were arriving by steamer and landing at the harbour for the short walk along the promenade and into town. Their numbers had greatly increased with the arrival of the railway from Watchet. Despite the great expansion in the overall national economy and the appearance of steam vessels, the number of ships working to and from the harbour had dropped to single figures, mostly smacks or sloops, and mostly on the lingering routes to and from Bristol and South Wales.

A factor in this situation was that, unlike its former rival at Bridgwater, Minehead had a relatively sparse hinterland. It did have a lifeboat station, one of the later ones, and it made a number of rescues, mainly of local fishing boats. There was also some local shipbuilding in a small yard west of the harbour, but that closed down in the early 1800s. The 80-ton schooner *Perriton* was built on the beach around 1881, but that ended another maritime activity.

By the 1900s small vessels were still using Minehead harbour, but only on an occasional and irregular basis. Somewhat larger vessels registered there continued

An overall view of Minehead Harbour with a ketch moored at the quay.

Modern Minehead, its links with seafaring maintained by a collection of pleasure craft and a few surviving fishing vessels.

working in the Bristol Channel with jobbing cargoes to and from Bristol, coal and limestone from South Wales and the odd loads of bricks, tiles and the like, but the volume of traffic on offer was declining, siphoned off by larger steam and motor vessels, railways and then road transport. Excursions steamers brought increasing numbers of holidaymakers instead.

The Ridler vessel *Orestes* brought in the Welsh coal supplies until the middle of the 1930s. This traffic continued after the war in the hands of Captain Rawle, one-time Minehead harbour master, and owner of one of the last local trading vessels, the lovely 56-ton ketch *Emma Louise*. She had originally been built in 1883 by John Westacott and was the final vessel he built in the Barnstaple yard before moving to the Torridge. Starting her life as a 66-ton topsail schooner, *Emma Louise* was subsequently converted to a ketch rig in the quite common pursuit of cutting crewing costs. After getting new masts and a new 80hp engine in 1948 she was sold to new owners at Braunton and her work taken over by the iron ketch *Mary Stewart* which did five years on the coal run. But that, to all intents and purposes, was the end of the traditional cargo activity at Minehead, and the waters of the harbour became exclusive to fishing boats and leisure craft.

A build-up of shingle at the harbour mouth in the 1940s led to its closure in 1947 but this shingle obstacle was cleared. The harbour property then passed from the Luttrell interests to the urban district council in 1951 for a token payment of £2 and, as the memories of war died away and a measure of peacetime prosperity took its place, the harbour could move into its new leisure role and increasingly provide an anchorage for small yachts and motor cruisers. The harbour area still remains a microcosm of a fine little port with its walls intact, warehouse building still there and, behind, the inevitable limekilns which once had taken cargoes of limestone from Aberthaw and culm from Saundersfoot. All just sufficient to give a small impression of the trading activity that would once have taken place there.

Porlock Weir
On several occasions before the end of the first millennium, Danish raiding parties landed on the shores of Porlock Bay and attacked the small settlement

The Pool at Porlock Weir where cargo vessels used to have to wait for sufficient water to enter the small dock beyond.

at Porlock proper. Their long boats would have been drawn up on the shingle
which was just a short march away. Five hundred years later they could have
landed further along the shingle at Porlock Weir where new habitation was
growing up around the entrance to a small stream coming down from the heights
of Porlock Hill. There, nicely sheltered by the western arm of the bay, the tiny
estuary was converted into a simple, but effective, little harbour. To supply the
local area and distribute its produce small local vessels were sailing to and from
the other Bristol Channel harbours, to other west coast ports and also to Ireland
and Europe. Others fished the local waters.

By the early nineteenth century the natural shingle bank had become the outer
face of a small dock, enclosed by 30ft gates to retain the waters of the incoming
tide and with a quay and warehouse facilities on the inland side. With a good
depth of water and cottages nearby for mariners and coastguards, the small facility
dealt with lime for the adjacent limekiln, culm to fire it and coal for the larger
population at Porlock itself. It might have had a much busier existence had the

Two motor fishing vessels are moored just inside the tiny dock at Porlock Weir. The single
gate of the lock entrance and the former coastguard cottages can also be seen.

plans to make it the terminus of a railway bringing iron ore down from Exmoor for the South Wales smelters ever come to fruition.

Porlock Weir vessels were sailing across to Wales and Ireland as early as the 1500s and over the centuries a variety of small trading craft were based there. They ranged in size from the 37ft ex-Pill pilot cutter *Auspicious* to the 85-ton French-built schooner *Flying Foam*. Such vessels brought in Welsh coal, sand and cement and some more general cargoes. Their outwards loads were mainly local products, bricks, bark and pit props from the Exmoor estates. The smack *John and William* was built on the flat piece of land behind the harbour in 1858, but no other shipbuilding activity is recorded. Over the years a number of local men owned vessels, some operating from Minehead and some in joint arrangements with others, but Porlock Weir was essentially a small facility, catering for local needs and produce and having only a small share in the wider shipping activity.

The last traditional sailing into Porlock Weir was in 1950 when the 71ft *Democrat* brought in a load of coal. Sadly she herself was nearing the end of her working life and sank while on a voyage to Jersey four years later. The long history of fishing is kept alive by a few local boatmen, but the attractive small harbour is now used mainly by yachtsmen and has accommodation and shops nearby to serve the needs of holidaymakers.

PART 3 Sail Gives Way

9. THE YEARS OF POWER

Attempts to apply steam power to ships date back to the 1770s. In this country a curious twin-hulled vessel with a two-cylinder atmospheric engine was tried successfully on Dalswinton Loch in 1788, achieving 5mph over a short distance. However, the real breakthrough was still fourteen years ahead. It came in the March of 1802 when a 56ft-long vessel, with a double stern and a single paddle wheel between, made a momentous trip on the Forth & Clyde Canal. The vessel was the *Charlotte Dundas* and it successfully towed two fully-loaded 70-ton sloops for nearly 20 miles in six hours and despite a contrary wind.

The great limitation of the sailing vessel was its total dependence on wind and tides and the success of *Charlotte Dundas* not only heralded an easement of this constraint but also pointed in the direction in which the early application of steam power was to go.

By the 1820s small paddle steamers were to be seen in all the major British estuaries, many of them originating from the growing Clyde shipbuilding industry. Slowly the early side-lever engines became more reliable and the idea of a stern paddle gave way to the side location of two separate paddles, a move which reduced linkage complications and increased vessel manoeuvrability. Bristol shared in the early haste to employ paddle steamers, initially in towing sailing ships up the tidal and navigationally tricky River Avon, a trend which was to spell the end of the traditional towage by hobblers whose homes and large rowing boats were centred on Pill.

By the middle of the century the steam boats serving Bristol were not only towing vessels along the Avon, but were also the foundation of a whole network of packet boat operation. The city enjoyed regular packet boat services to Chepstow, Cardiff, Newport, Neath, Swansea, Carmarthen, Tenby, Ilfracombe,

Milford Haven, Hayle and Padstow, and further afield to Liverpool, Dublin, Cork and Waterford. It also had its own local 'commuter' service between the Cumberland Basin, at the entrance to the floating harbour, and Portishead. On this route the *Fairy Queen* was operating a daily trip each way, sometimes two if the tide was right, at times varying from 7 a.m. to 4.30 p.m. depending on the depth of water available in the Avon. In one direction *Fairy Queen* called at Pill and in the other at the Lamplighters landing stage at Shirehampton. A day ticket for the whole journey cost one and sixpence in a best cabin (two shillings return) and one shilling in a second cabin.

On the high seas steam was initially confined to an auxiliary role owing to the limitations of bunkering. Carrying coal meant sacrificing paying cargo space and arranging overseas supplies for refuelling on the journey meant further costs and complications. Even so, steam power continued to gain ground in new ship construction, but it was not a simple displacement. For one thing a seagoing vessel of any sort could have quite a long life and, in the case of wooden sailing vessels, be relatively easy of repair. Lightly abandoning such assets did not make economic sense. Furthermore, early steam engines were very liable to break down and their use, especially in managing the firebox and boiler, demanded new handling skills which took time to acquire. A steam vessel required an engineer as well as its other hands. And an engine of any size would need a separate hand to handle the coal, fuel the firebox and keep the steam pressure at a sufficient level. All of which added to costs.

The middle of the nineteenth century saw the steam paddle tug, initially with a wooden hull, but later of iron, firmly entrenched in a useful towing role. Bridgwater got its first steam tug in 1837 and another in 1840. Ten years on and tugs were participating regularly in the pleasure trip market which was expanding rapidly in the Bristol Channel. The Bristol tugs had set the trend by the simple expedient of installing temporary extra decking, seating and awnings. And they went wherever they could find this useful extra revenue, the Bristol tug *Alpha* operating an excursion from Uphill as early as 1843 and later visits to the little pill there being made by the *Air.*

In 1851 the Bridgwater Steam Towing Company's tug *Perseverance* emulated the example of these early excursion pioneers with a pleasure trip to Minehead that proved exceedingly popular. Three days later the pleasure seekers who joined another steamer trip, this time by the *Cardiff Castle*, were not so happy with the outcome. On the journey to Flat Holm, strong winds and heavy seas gave the party a very uncomfortable ride and the thirty-one brave souls who went ashore on the island had cause to regret their adventurous spirit when their steamer was unable to take them off and had to run to Cardiff for shelter. It was back to effect a rescue on the next day, but only after those marooned had spent a very hungry and uncomfortable night.

The Bridgwater Steam Towing Company in 1897 operated a tug which had been built the previous year in Sunderland, and named *Bonita*. She worked for the Sully coal interests whose stacking needs came to occupy a significant area alongside the enclosed dock and which had its own railway siding connection. The tug company sold its tug fleet just before the outbreak of the First World War and went into liquidation, but was revived in 1922 and continued to operate for another twelve years.

Screw propulsion was challenging paddle wheels before the nineteenth century reached its halfway point and steam tonnage finally exceeded that of sail in 1866. This situation was not the case in local waters and even as the new century dawned Somerset harbours would still display many more masts than funnels. Behind that appearance lies the fact that relatively compact and simple marine engines were becoming increasingly available and the natural course was to install one in any worthwhile trow or ketch that could find enough traffic to keep it busy. And, even if a vessel was not to be converted, towage readily was available at the busier places so that, either way, the old dependence on wind, weather and water was greatly reduced. The journey time improvements achieved could help fund the outlay on the new engine and the structural alterations needed for its installation.

A major and more general change was that brought about by the advent of small, reliable marine engines which ran on paraffin. Between the turn of the century and the outbreak of the First World War many vessels had one installed and became vastly easier to handle as a result. Installing a marine engine in a wooden hull was not an overcomplicated matter and relatively few sailing vessels were built with metal hulls in place of the traditional wood, especially as few smaller builders were able to convert their premises, tools and techniques.

The internal marine combustion engine certainly prolonged the life and work of the sailing coasters and where possible these engines were updated to give more power and more reliability as time passed. The Bridgwater ketch *Irene*, as one example, had her first engine fitted in 1919, a 40hp Invincible. In 1921 it was replaced by a 70hp Bolinder and in 1939 by a Ellwe Suenska engine. By 1979 she was using a Gardner diesel and was up-rated again in the 1980s with a 135hp engine. The ubiquitous Kelvin marine engine was first produced in Glasgow in 1908 and subsequent models have been used extensively since that time. Kelvin is still producing marine engines.

When the end of hostilities did not bring the hoped-for world of plenty, more vessels were motorised in the 1920s in a bid to hold on to traditional traffics in the face of a new threat from the motor lorry and from a surplus of redundant shipping. But the sailing vessels still around were all getting older and easily ousted by more modern coasting vessels in the competition for what waterborne traffic remained. By 1920 two-thirds of the vessels visiting the Parrett were steamships or motor vessels. Steam, too, however improved and refined, was also on the way out, but when the surviving movements to Portishead, Highbridge, Bridgwater and the various town coal boat destinations finally petered out, a new era was still to occur.

Surviving to keep alive the seafaring traditions of the Somerset coast, the cargoes up the River Parrett to Dunball represented a modern revival. In 1995, for example, there were sixty-six of them, representing around 28,000 tons. In the following year there were seventy-four, and in 2000 a total of sixty-seven of which twenty-nine were coastal and the others foreign. In the latter year the total cargo tonnage handled by the Port of Bridgwater, which to all intents and purposes meant at Dunball, was 76,790 tons and this was 43 per cent up on the year before. Of this figure for the coastal business, some 29,620 tons was sand and stone, the remainder animal feed, granite, salt, timber anthracite and peat.

At the lowest point of the tide a steam collier sits on the mud alongside the upper reach of Highbridge Wharf. To the left is a line of railway wagons and the route of the single line to Burnham and ahead the site of the sea lock of the ill-fated Glastonbury Canal.

Dunball Wharf at the turn of the century was operated by A.G. Watts who provided wharfage, cranage, storage and distribution facilities there. ARC (Southern) Ltd was running the adjacent sand terminal at that time. Information about arrivals was passed by them to the harbour master based at Burnham who would contact the incoming vessel by VHF radio when it arrived at the Gore Buoy, usually about two-and-a-half hours before high tide – normally a spring to provide adequate water depth in the river. Monitored on a radar screen, the ship's master would then bring his vessel to the agreed point for picking up the harbour master or one of his assistants who would then act as pilot along the river. Another of the responsibilities of the harbour master was that of monitoring the river channel which was forever changing.

The length limit for vessels heading for Dunball was normally considered to be 77m, but an 88m vessel could be handled if necessary and provided it was

The *Marc Trader*, a modern vessel with hydraulic superstructure which can be lowered to pass beneath bridges, approaches Dunball Wharf in the time-honoured manner of turning into the tide.

A Lapthorn coal vessel, *Hoo Plover*, awaits unloading to the quay stack at Dunball Wharf. Stored Bristol Channel sand, brought in to the inlet at the end of the quay, can also be seen.

one of the new breed of sea/river vessels with a shallow draught and, usually, a telescopic wheelhouse. Typical of the incoming vessels of that period was the *Marc Trader*, a 1,301-ton general cargo carrier, 75m long and built in 1983 at Papenburg. Equipped with six-cylinder, 600bhp Deutz 4SA oil engines, she has a thrust propeller forward as well as the conventional stern housing.

Sedgemoor District Council had become the 'Competent Harbour Authority' in 1988 when it took over the Port of Bridgwater from Trinity House and became responsible for providing pilotage services for all boats over 30m long. This requirement derives from the constant changes in the navigable channel and the current and tidal extremes with the pilotage services carried out by the harbour master/pilot and three relief pilots. The District Council's responsibilities include not only pilotage and safety but also maintaining navigational aids and keeping the lower Parrett clear of obstructions, waste and spillage.

In more recent years the traffic pattern at Dunball has changed somewhat with marine sand and gravel dredged in the Bristol Channel rising to account for some two-thirds of the arriving tonnage and salt much of the remainder. The sand wharf passed into the hands of Hanson Aggregates Ltd while the main wharf was acquired by River Bulk Shipping. Discounting the occasional use of the roll-on roll-off berth at Combwich for heavy items for British Electric at Hinkley, Dunball came to be the last traditional Somerset cargo port to survive into the twenty-first century.

10. DECLINE AND PRESERVATION

The pattern of the last years of cargo sailing vessels is one of gradual decline precipitated by economic change, increasing rail and road competition and the impact of major wars. This pattern in the Bristol Channel mirrored similar changes in coastal shipping elsewhere and was only slowed, rather than reversed by the increasing use of steam and oil engines for propulsion. Certainly these had a major impact as is clear from records which show some of the incredibly lengthy journey times inflicted on sailing vessels by bad weather. In good conditions, it might be possible to get from Bridgwater to Rotterdam in ten days, but one journey to Padstow took as many as fifty!

Nearly all the remaining schooners and ketches had been converted to the use of an engine by the mid to late 1930s. By this time economies of scale were prompting a move away from small manufacturing units to large scale production demanding bulk movement and more sophisticated distribution, for which road transport proved greatly more flexible and effective. Bulk cargoes like coal continued to be on offer for water carriage, but as steamships and a new generation of motor vessels increased in size to curb costs and freight rates, the older wooden vessels had found themselves less and less welcome at busy ports using modern loading and unloading equipment. Other factors impinged on the situation, albeit less directly, and these included rising educational standards and the availability of easier jobs ashore.

The requisitioning of a large number of the commercial sailing fleet in both world wars led to losses and deterioration. Of some thirty Bridgwater coasters in 1913, no less than two-thirds were subsequently lost, sunk, wrecked or reported missing. In the second great conflict many of the vessels used as barrage balloon anchorage in naval harbours, for example, were beyond commercial repair when hostilities ended. Reparation was not enough to build new vessels even if that would have been commercially viable. Another sad cost of the two major conflicts was not just the vessels themselves, but a terrible price in human lives and thus of experienced seamen.

The demise of wooden vessels was marked further in the South West when building ended with the launching of the ketch *Irene* at Bridgwater in 1907 followed by the schooner *Garlandstone* at Calstock on the Tamar. The latter was on the building stocks for several years before its launch in 1909, the shipyard by this time doing mainly repair work, and construction on the new boat being undertaken during slack periods to keep the workforce employed.

The continuing development of road transport permitted by the appearance of more efficient road vehicles and, at the same time, the competition from small steel motor coasters gathered pace in the 1920s and 1930s so that cargoes for wooden sailing vessels became even more difficult to find. Many of the remaining trows suffered the indignity of becoming dumb lighters in the larger docks, e.g. Gloucester and Bristol, some of them lasting there into the 1960s. Many other sailing vessels, including the schooners and ketches, were hulked in the estuaries and rivers of the South West. Very few rivers do not have the bones of some past sailing vessel. The estuary of the Taw and Torridge has the remains of many fine sailors, but the banks of the Severn at Purton is a veritable 'elephants' graveyard' where the remains of nearly all the types of wooden vessels that plied the Bristol Channel have been deliberately hulked to stabilise the area between the River Severn and the banks of the Gloucester & Sharpness Canal.

The Purton remains have recently been recorded and in most cases identified. Each has its own remarkable story. The trow *Severn Collier*, for example, spent her life serving the Cadbury chocolate factory at Frampton-on-Severn. Her regular cargo was about 100 tons of coal from Princess Royal Colliery in the Forest of Dean and the intention had been to load this at Lydney, cross to Sharpness and then move up the canal to Frampton. Taking eight hours to make the crossing proved her underpowered so the cross-river movement was made by rail across the Severn Bridge to Sharpness. There the counter-balanced coal chute was used to tip the wagons and allow their load to fill the trow, which then completed the journey up to Frampton. The wrecking of the Severn Bridge by out-of-control tankers on the river brought this fifty-year saga to an end.

Over the centuries of sail, re-usable material would have been salvaged from vessels which had reached the end of their life. Dedicated shipbreaking to this end took place at several locations, including Clevedon and Uphill, but sailing ships wrecked on rocks or beaches tended just to be left for the tides to erode them. There are examples near Portishead Pier and on Berrow Beach. At Dunball the ketch *Fame* ran into the riverbank opposite the wharf in 1915 and was abandoned because she could not be shifted. Another ketch, the *Trio*, was wrecked near Combwich during a stormy March in 1939 and the *SS Tender* was brought up to Dunball in 1943, stripped of her boilers and other fittings, and then left to rot there.

The last resting place of the old trow *Harriet* after ending her working days as an Ashmead dumb barge in the City Docks at Bristol. The vessel is among several used to stabilise the land strip between the River Severn and the Gloucester & Sharpness Canal. (Roy Gallop)

The fate of the *Trio* is a reminder that the passage of the years and the changing face of trade and transport were not the only enemies of both local vessels and any seagoing craft frequenting the Somerset coastal waters. Storm and tempest, collisions and carelessness have all played their part and a few gaunt timbers can still be seen as a stark reminder of this. The wreck on the beach at Berrow is a prime example. Visible at low water after over a century, she was the wooden Norwegian barque *Nornen*, a victim of severe gales in March 1897. These put a steamer and a schooner on the Dunball Sands, sent three colliers outbound from the River Parrett back there to shelter and stranded the ketches *Magnet* and *Good Templar*. The *Nornen* was not so fortunate. After seeking shelter in Lundy Roads in an attempt to ride out the storm she was remorselessly driven back until grounded on the tail of Gore Sands. The Burnham rowing lifeboat took off the

In addition to changes in the pattern of trade and competition, age and accident also reduced the numbers of trading vessels in the Bristol Channel, most now forgotten, but some still in their last resting place, like these rotting timbers near the pier at Portishead.

crew after they had attempted to moor the vessel, but successive tides and high winds drove her further up the wide beach. Subsequent attempts to lighten and refloat the barque proved unsuccessful and she was subsequently sold for such of her timbers as could be salvaged. Various souvenirs passed into local hands and the remainder weathered over the years to remain a reminder that sailing will always have its hazards.

Three well-known hulks were deemed a nuisance at Uphill, on the beach across the Axe from Brean Down. They had been abandoned on the saltings and had become infested with rats. The Borough Council had to take on responsibility for disposing of them and they were eventually auctioned in 1939. The *R.D. Passmore* made £4 2s 6d, and the *Daisy* went for £5 0s 0d. The *Nora* did not find a purchaser and a year later was deliberately set on fire to release her scrap iron.

The 1897 wreck of the barque *Nornen* on Berrow Sands. The vessel was driven ashore in a severe gale, but all her crew survived. (Roy Gallop)

And so the twentieth century progressed. Very few vessels had returned to the trade after the Second World War, all but a very few were auxiliaries rather than conventional sailing craft by this time and by the 1960s it was all over. Some of the schooners and ketches in better condition were sold to foreign owners where a living could be made in an easier environment.

Happily, three wooden sailing schooners and ketches have been preserved in the South West and are part of the maritime heritage scene. The *Garlandstone* is now restored and moored at Morwellham Quay, a heritage site on the Tamar River. The *Irene* can frequently be seen in Bristol Docks, but sails regularly to other ports and European maritime festivals. The *Kathleen and May*, the last three-masted schooner to trade in British waters, has been the subject of more than one restoration project and was based at East the Water, Bideford, on the Torridge

River. Only one trow has survived, the *Spry*. Built in Chepstow in 1894 she was a Lower/Middle Severn trader working in the Bristol Channel and up to Worcester until 1950. She is now in the care of the Ironbridge Gorge Museum where she has been restored.

In addition to the achievements in the preservation of these typical cargo sailing vessels, recent years have also featured a good deal of restoration work and the building of new craft to traditional designs. Fittingly, Bristol is the scene of a lot of this type of work which, in its way perpetuates the spirit that built the *SS Great Britain* there in the first place and then returned it to its original resplendent condition, a feat that many who saw the rotting hulk arrive home from the Falklands must have thought well-nigh impossible.

This same regard for its maritime heritage saw work started in 1994 on a replica of the caravel *Matthew*, the vessel that John Cabot commanded on his epic voyage to Newfoundland. Built to celebrate the 500th anniversary of that achievement, the vessel was designed by the naval architect Colin Mudie and was built by Storm Sail Services, precursor to the Bristol Classic Boat Company. She was launched into Bristol's floating harbour in time to take part in the first International Festival of the Sea held there in 1996 and in the same year made a trip across the Atlantic to Newfoundland and back. Her route on this momentous recreation of an important historic event took the *Matthew* down the Bristol Channel and along the course on which so many Somerset vessels had plied their trade in earlier times. The vessel is still based in Bristol, but actively sails to many European ports.

The Bristol Classic Boat Company, R.B. Boatbuilders and Tim Loftus Boatbuilding are three Bristol firms building and restoring classical sailing vessel types in the city's floating harbour. In this process they are using traditional methods, skills and materials, including locally sourced timber, larch planking and copper fastenings. A design prominent in this activity due to its superb and well proven sailing qualities is that of the Bristol Channel pilot cutter.

The Bristol Channel pilot cutters were replaced by steam cutters in 1912 and most of them were sold on as yachts. Their excellent sea-keeping qualities and speed made them ideal conversions. Some of these original vessels are still active; *Mascotte*, *Olga* and *Carriad* are still sailing. Another original is the *Peggy*, owned by Mr Diccon Pridie, based in Bristol docks and still doing annual cruises. She was built by the well-known Pill shipwright Edwin Rowles in 1903 for the pilot Arthur Case and converted to a yacht in the 1920s. *Peggy*'s original name was *Wave* and she carried the number ten on her mainsail.

So well regarded is this pilot cutter design that there have been a number of new builds in Bristol in recent years. A notable example of these was the *Pegasus* which was completed at the yard of the Bristol Classic Boat Company for the

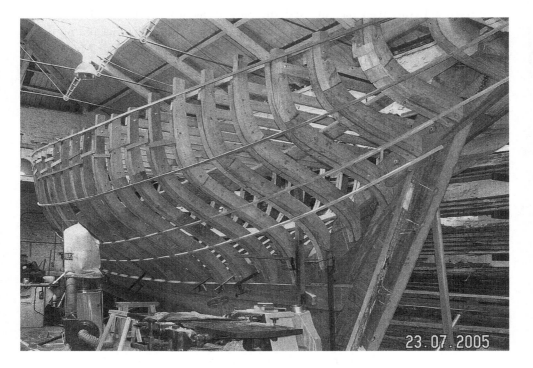

An example of the renaissance of the traditional small sailing vessel, the grace of the old Bristol Channel pilot cutters is very evident in this new build being undertaken in the Underfall Yard at Bristol in 2005. (Roy Gallop)

Island Sailing Trust, a charity which has a small fleet of well-tried sailing vessels for the sail training of young people. With oak frames and larch planking, *Pegasus* is 74ft long, has a beam of 14ft 9in and a draught of 8ft 6in. Based in Plymouth she takes a proud part in the Tall Ships Race.

At the Underfall Yard in Bristol City Docks R.B. Boatbuilders have, in the last ten years, built a further three pilot cutters for sailing charter work. *Edith Gray* is 38ft 6in long, with a beam of 11ft 6in and a draught of 7ft 6in. Using larch on oak with a transom stern she is with Wild Sailing. The slightly larger *Morwenna* is 45ft long, has the same beam width and a draught the smaller by just an inch. The third member of the trio, *Mischief*, is of similar construction and is based on the lines of the vessel made famous by the writer and explorer W.H. Tilman who used former pilot cutters in his voyages to extreme locations in the Arctic and Antarctic regions.

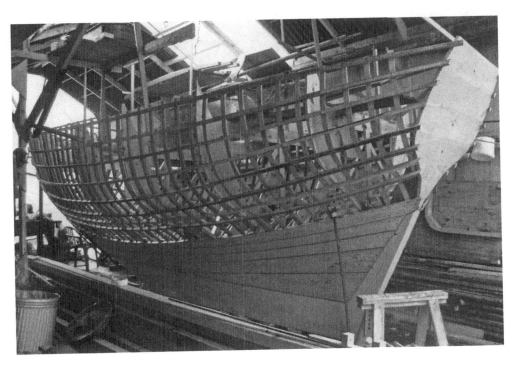

Another new-build to a traditional design, this hull in the Bristol Yard of Tim Loftus Boatbuilding shows the fine transom stern, and the build-up from the keel of larch planking on oak frames fixed with copper nails. (Roy Gallop)

In the same yard at the time of writing is the old pilot cutter *Breeze* which was built by Coopers of Pill for the Cardiff pilot Albert Cope in 1887–88. After starting work out of Cardiff in that year she was then owned by the same family until the steam cutters took over around 1912. *Breeze* is probably the second-oldest vessel of her type still in existence and the only remaining example of one built by Coopers of Pill. With a deck length of 38ft and a 12ft beam she was surveyed in Porlock Weir back in 1992 and was then afloat and in commission, but by 2006 she was on the quay and in poor condition. Seven years later *Breeze* was housed in R.B. Boatbuilders' yard undergoing a careful restoration which paid the maximum regard to her traditional construction based on sawn oak frames with larch planking, wooden trenails and iron dumps.

The predecessors of these preserved and restored vessels had long and active lives and with good care and maintenance these recent additions could last until

At the Underfall Yard of R.B. Boatbuilders, the former pilot cutter *Breeze* awaits the restoration that will give her a new lease of life. (Roy Gallop)

An old ketch lies on the mud at Bideford Quay, nursing a broken bowsprit but still looking as if she might one day put to sea again. (Roy Gallop)

Proudly showing just what can be achieved the ketch *Irene*, now beautifully restored, is pictured here in the floating harbour at Bristol.

the twenty-second century. So all is not lost. The honourable tradition of cargo carrying in wooden sailing vessels that enriched and shaped the communities around the Severn and the Bristol Channel has a superb and tangible memorial in these preserved, restored and new-build vessels and designs. They have become part of a rich heritage of the many older vessels preserved at ports and harbours all around Great Britain.

APPENDIX I

Ship Arrivals at Dunball Wharf December 1904

Date	Vessels
1st	*Charles, Mary, Galley*
2nd	*Caroline, Ring Dove*
3rd	*Champion, Fanny Jane*
4th	*Flora, Robin Hood, Theodore*
5th	A-1 Steamship
6th	*Victory*
7th	*Conquest*
8th	*Mary, Caroline, Sarah*
9th	*Shepherd*
10th	*Champion, Charles, William*
11th	*Eley*
12th	*Rival*
13th	*Ring Dove, Two Brothers*
18th	*Mary, Champion, Caroline, Victory*
19th	*Martin Luther*
20th	*Sarah, Charles, Fame*
21st	*Jonadab*
24th	*Champion, William, Palace*
25th	*Longrey Lass*
29th	*Charles*

Multiple Visits:-

Two	*William*	10th and 24th
	Ring Dove	2nd and 13th
	Sarah	8th and 20th
Three	*Mary*	1st, 8th and 18th
	Caroline	2nd, 8th and 18th
	Charles	10th, 20th and 29th
Four	*Champion*	3rd, 8th, 10th and 24th

GLOSSARY

Adze	Axe-like tool with curved blade used for shaping wood.
Bath Bricks	Renowned scouring blocks manufactured from silica sediment found in the River Parrett at Bridgwater.
Boom	Pivoted spar fixed to the mast at one end and to which the foot of the sail is attached.
Carvel-built	Wooden vessels constructed with the hull planks fitted edge-to-edge to create a smooth surface.
Clinker-built	Wooden vessels with hull planks overlapping, resulting in a much lighter construction than when carvel-built.
Coamings	The raised sides of the hatches onto which the hatch covers are fitted, also increasing longitudinal strength.
Counter stern	The after part of the hull projecting beyond the stern post.
Culm	Low grade, small coal, usually anthracite.
Dumps	Large iron nails of square section, nowadays galvanised.
Eroder	Boat with pumps for removing sediment and vegetation from rivers, docks and harbours.
Flatner	Simple, planked, flat-bottomed boat for use in shallow waters.
Gaff	Spar to which the head of a fore and aft sail is attached.
Gunwale	Raised deck edging around the hull.
Halyards	Ropes for hauling up or lowering sails.
Hard	Man-made sloped, even surface for loading or landing cargo to wheeled vehicles.
Keel	Barge with square sail found mainly in the Humber and connected waters.
Keelage	Fee charged by some ports to permit vessels to dock.
Knees	Bracket supports between frames and deck.
Land Waiter	Shore-based customs official responsible for enforcing import and export regulations and collecting import duties.
Letpass	Authority for British vessels and seamen to load or land at any creek or port in England and Wales.
Pill	Secondary waterway off a river or creek.

Rhyne	(pronounced rhine or rheen) Minor drainage channel.
Sheets	The ropes attached to and used for controlling the sails.
Shrouds	Ropes or wires from the ship's sides to the head of the mast to provide lateral support.
Slime batches	Collecting areas for the sediment used for Bath Bricks.
Smack	Ketch or cutter used mainly for fishing.
Spar	Yard or mast of a ship.
Strakes	The hull planking of a vessel.
Transom	Flat stern.
Warp	Move a vessel by hauling on a fixed rope.
Warps	Ropes used for mooring.
Yawl	Two-masted sailing vessel with small mizzen mast set behind the rudder post.

INDEX

NOTE: Virtually all the pages in this work contain information on the movements of the cargoes carried by vessels using the Somerset ports and harbours. Coal is an outstanding example, passing as it did from Lydney, Newport, Cardiff, Neath and Swansea to every landing place along the Somerset coast right from the earliest days of shipping activity. Timber and livestock were also numerous and frequent cargoes. Specific cargo commodities are therefore excluded from this index for the sake of simplicity and effectiveness, but the sections of the book dealing with trade activity and ports, pills and wharves, together with the diagram on page 25, provide general information on the various types of cargo carried and the routes it followed.

INDEX OF VESSELS

Lightning Source UK Ltd.
Milton Keynes UK
UKOW07f1622121214

243051UK00004B/65/P